JANE KIDD is particularly well-qualified to write this book. She comes from a family of horsemen and journalists (her grandfather was Lord Beaverbrook).

She graduated with an honours degree in Economics and Politics from Bristol University. She was also a member of Junior and Adult British Show Jumping Teams, and as a junior was twice a member of teams that won the European Show Jumping Championships.

Jane Kidd has written six other books, has worked as an editor in part-work publishing and is a regular contributor to the equestrian press in Britain and America.

A riding accident prevented her continuing her show jumping career, but she is an active participant in dressage riding. She is an Official British Horse Society judge, and organises the annual Hickstead Dressage Championships.

Jane Kidd lives and works at her family-run Maple Stud in Surrey, where she breeds competition horses, using Hanoverian stallions to thoroughbred mares.

HORSEMANSHIP
IN
EUROPE

HORSEMANSHIP
IN
EUROPE

JANE KIDD

Foreword by Colonel Sir Mike Ansell

J. A. ALLEN
LONDON

ISBN o 85131 243 8

Published in 1977 by J. A. Allen & Company Limited,
1 Lower Grosvenor Place,
London, SW1W oEL.

Book production by Bill Ireson.

Set in 11/13 Monotype Garamond, printed and bound by
Billing & Sons Limited, Guildford, London and Worcester.

FOREWORD

by Colonel Sir Mike Ansell

I FEEL sure that this book of Jane Kidd's about breeding, training and competing in Europe will be of great interest to many.

In Europe training has been taken more seriously than in Britain, every rider learning some dressage, which really only means training and developing the natural movements of the horse. In Britain, especially in the pre-war days the word dressage was usually connected with the circus. The majority of riders went hunting and most were only too happy to get to the end of the hunt, however many tumbles they had. However in the Army we were taught to train our horses, and as a result had the more pleasure both in the hunting field and on the polo ground.

I was fortunate that in the years from 1931 I had the opportunity to use my leave to go each year to work with the Cadre Noir at Saumur. I learned the value and the more important factor the joy of riding a well trained horse. Personally when at Saumur with the Cadre Noir and riding a horse which had been fourth at the Olympic Games in dressage, I used to wonder why I played polo and hunted. I had so much pleasure riding a trained horse.

Later in company with Colonel Williams, having been to Saumur we went to the Belgian, Dutch and German Cavalry Schools. At all these schools we learned that methods of training must be adapted to the type and breeding of the horse. The really great horsemen demand what they wish but adapt their methods to the type of horse they are riding.

I sincerely hope many will read Jane Kidd's book, and learn more about horsemanship in Europe. If they can find out how to allow their horse to maintain his character and personality, how much more pleasure they will have.

MIKE ANSELL

CONTENTS

LIST OF ILLUSTRATIONS

INTRODUCTION

BRITAIN's membership of the Common Market has led to an examination of our systems and institutions. Comparisons between them and those on the Continent have helped to show where improvements can be made. It occurred to me that such an examination should not be limited to industry, trade unions, education and the like, but should include my greatest interest, equestrianism. Europe, I thought, must be full of information and ideas that could help and interest British horsemen. I resolved to visit Europe and this book is the outcome of my journey.

I set off intending to make an examination of the ideas and methods of the trainers the central feature of my book, but I found training methods could not be properly understood in isolation.

In each country training methods evolve from the character of the citizen, from the type of horse they breed to ride and from the form of competitions they hold. A fascinating picture built up for each country. The type of people and country was reflected in the character of the horse they bred, the methods by which they chose to ride them and in the system they organised for riding.

I have followed this concept in my book. For each country I have tried to set the scene, to describe a little of the atmosphere I felt when there, the attitude of the people towards their horses, the history of the horse in their country and their successes with him. Then I have considered the type of warmblood (riding) horse they have chosen to breed and the system they have created to do so. I have also discussed how the various countries use the horse. For most Europeans it is within a club system. I have looked at such systems in each country, discussed their varying functions, facilities and approach to riding.

The trainers, however, were my greatest interest and their ideas, methods and approach were more easily understood with this

background established; as were the differences between individuals in each country and between the nationalities themselves.

The value of each country's equestrian institutions and trainers
must be judged in the competitive sphere. I looked at the types
and numbers of competitions held, the rewards given, the amount
of professionalism, the famous participants and the country's
international standing in all aspects of equestrianism.

My picture of each country was made by interviewing, by
watching and questioning and, wherever possible, by being
trained myself. I have tried to tie together a host of impressions,
facts and ideas, to give some understanding of the horsemen of
Europe. I have also collected information for that increasing
number of people who go to the Continent. Although this cannot
be a comprehensive coverage, I hope it will give European
bound riders, purchasers or equestrian minded tourists, an idea
of where their interests might be met.

For those who are staying at home, I hope this book will give
them some insight into European ideas and methods which
increasingly affect our own lives. I also hope that it may help to
broaden the horizons of the horse world and perhaps to persuade
more people of the value and enjoyment of European travel.

I chose the countries which have the best reputations for their
trainers, their schools and their horses and which are relatively
close to Britain. But this examination has been an enthralling
adventure and I am restless now to find out what happens further
afield.

CHAPTER ONE

FRANCE

THE French are the world's greatest contributors to the art of riding. Before the French directed their energies to it, riding was treated as an instinctive activity. In over three centuries they turned it into an exercise which could be approached rationally. They showed that force could be replaced by logical methods of training, and in doing so they laid the foundations of modern equitation.

Although nearly all the credit for the modern approach to equestrianism must go to the French, it was an Italian who completed the first book. Frederico Grisone in 1550 wrote about the techniques of dressage. The aristocracy of Europe were impressed, and clamoured to find out how to make their horses perform High School movements. Indoor riding schools were built at the major residences of the royalty and nobility. France became the undisputed equestrian leader and Versailles, the most lavish home of any European monarch, the most famous school in these equestrian developments.

In the imposing surroundings of Versailles and in the manèges of Paris, the classical methods of training horse and rider were formalised. Force became less and less necessary, as techniques of co-operation were developed. Many books were produced but it was the *écuyer* for the Paris Academy, who in 1733 wrote the most famous of all. *Ecole de Cavalerie* was the work of de la Guerinière and the principles he laid down are still adhered to by the custodians of the art of classical dressage, the Spanish Riding School at Vienna.

The Napoleonic wars brought an end to the decorative era of the Versailles School, but still France remained a major influence on the development of riding. Saumur, the home of the French cavalry, became the great equitation school of the nineteenth century. Books were produced by its *écuyers*, including General L'Hotte's *Questions Equestres*.

But the cavalry had to vie with civilians for equestrian influence. Riding exhibitions were popular forms of entertainment in those days and great circus riders emerged to challenge the principles and methods developed at Saumur. Again, the most important of these were French, notably Baucher, and also Fillis who grew up in France, although he was born in England.

By the beginning of the twentieth century the French equestrian masters had done their work. Over a period of three centuries they had developed and formalised the art of riding. It is their ideas and methods which with a few modifications form the basis of everything every rider is taught today.

It was appropriate, with this equestrian inheritance, that France was the first country to stage today's ultimate test in competitive horsemanship – the Olympic Equestrian Games. It was France who lobbied, successfully, for the inclusion of three jumping events in the 1900 Paris Games. These were Prize Jumping, Long Jumping and High Jump. The home team carried off many medals at these, and all the pre-First World War Olympic Games.

In the inter-war period the French vied with Sweden and Germany for the major dressage honours. Colonel Lesage, the individual winner in 1932 became famous for his loose rein piaff and was probably the most renowned exponent of the French style of dressage.

The Second World War marked the end of over three centuries of French supremacy in the art of dressage. Their swan song was in 1948 when they won a team gold medal in the Olympics, held at Wembley. They also won a silver individual medal but that was the end. The great heritage of French riding was dissipated. The international dressage arenas were no longer dominated by those flamboyant Frenchmen, whose free way of riding turned their horses into a means of art rather than machines.

The show jumping arenas did, if spasmodically, have the fun of seeing dashing Frenchmen run away with some glory. D'Orgiex the present French national trainer took an individual bronze medal at Wembley in 1948. D'Oriola galloped flat out around the jump off course in 1952 at the Helsinki Olympics to win the gold. Then there were 12 years in the doldrums before the maestro D'Oriola re-appeared to take a gold at Tokyo. He was also a member of the team who won the silver. Another member of that team was a fragile looking teenager, Janou Lefebvre. She was the youngest competitor in the Tokyo Games, and she later helped another French team to win a silver medal in Mexico. In 1970 at Copenhagen and 1974 at La Baule she won individual distinction by taking the Ladies World Championship.

Eventing has had an equally erratic record for the French, since the end of the Second World War. A French team won a bronze medal in Rome in 1960 and 8 years later in Mexico, Jean-Jacques Guyon earned on Pitou the individual gold. But these successes were startling in so far as they were not preceded or followed by further victories. It seems that recent French equestrian history is notable for flashes of outstanding riding and glorious results of which the winning of the 1976 team gold medal in show jumping was typical; but which cannot be maintained. The colourful stars of French riding seem to reflect the characteristics of their nation's history since the revolution – brilliant and talented but neither consistent or stable.

THE HORSE

France cannot blame her periods in the doldrums upon lack of horses as she has more than in any other western European country. They have too, areas in the country where the soil and climate are some of the best in the world for horse breeding.

The French have adopted as rational an approach to breeding as they did to riding. They have used their intellect to produce a horse suitable for their character and needs.

The thoroughbred was the first to gain them an international reputation. The English were astounded when, in 1865, Gladiateur crossed the Channel to wrest the triple crown from the originators of the thoroughbred race. Since then French thoroughbreds have won every important race, and they have formed the basis of racing stock in many other countries. The trotter, too, has been systematically bred since the beginning of this century, and is now a world class animal. In competition, however, the

French have used a wide variety of horses, including thoroughbreds, Anglo-Arabs, and the warmbloods the Anglo-Normans,
Bretons and Charolais.

After the Second World War, the French decided to tidy up
matters and to approach the breeding of competition horses in
the same way as they had done trotters and racehorses; to specifically set about producing, on a national scale, a horse for both
competition and riding. It was to be called the Cheval de Selle
Français. A Stud Book was started for this breed. It was to
cover all horses suitable for competitive work which meant that
all warmblood animals could apply for entry and even those which
had previously had their own name and stud book became known
as the Selle Français. These various breeds of warmbloods were
derived, as in the rest of Europe, from crosses between pure
breds (thoroughbreds, Arabs and Anglo-Arabs) and the indigenous work horses. In 1970 the types of sire of the Selle Français
were as follows:

> 33% were thoroughbred
> 20% were Anglo-Arab
> 45% were Selle Français, and
> 2% were trotter.

The Selle Français are the descendants of the work horses of
France, differing in type according to area, soil, climate and the
original stock used. Recently these various breeds of work horses
have been crossed with finer blood strains to meet the increasing
demand for riding horses. These cross-bred, but pedigree,
horses form the newly named race of Cheval de Selle Français.

These regional breeds included the Breton, originally a very
tough, stocky horse. However, as a result of frequent crossbreeding with thoroughbreds the Breton is now, what the French
call, A.Q.P.S., a horse that is very close to thoroughbred. Further
inland, in the Anjou area, is the Angevin and in the estuary of
the Loire is the Vendeen. Along the Loire, and in the departments
of Cher and Loire, is the home of the Charolais, and further south
towards the Massif Central there is the Limousin.

Normandy, bordering on the English Channel, has the largest
horse population. The soil there is rich in lime and iron, the
climate is similar to that of Britain, making it an excellent breeding

PLATE 1

Colonel St. André, the former *écuyer en chef* of the Cadre Noir congratulates his protégé Patrick le Rolland.

PLATE 2
Pierre Jonquères d'Oriola, the show jumping hero of France and the only rider ever to have won two individual Olympic gold medals.

area. The horse of this region, the Anglo-Norman, dominates the Selle Français Stud Book. Hundreds of years ago it was a famous war horse, but Danish blood turned it into a carriage horse, and an importation of Norfolk trotters and thoroughbreds in the last century resulted in the modern Anglo-Norman. This breed has been France's premier warmblood, and breeds of other areas have used infusions of the Anglo-Norman blood. The result has been fewer and fewer distinguishing features between the breeds of northern France. Therefore, uniting under the title, the Selle Français, was a natural development as well as a wise step in the quest to produce a top-class riding horse.

In the south, the riding horses tend to be of a more flighty and elegant nature. Most are Arabs, or have Arab blood in them. The Anglo-Arab predominates a breed derived from mixtures of Arabs with either thoroughbreds, or the native mares of South-west France. These native mares have distinctive Oriental features and were said to be descendants of horses left after the Moslem invasion of some 1,200 years ago. Over the years battles and trade led to more Oriental stock being brought into France, adding speed and handiness to the toughness of the native horses.

Systematic breeding of the Anglo-Arab in France dates from the middle of the nineteenth century, when the Pompadour Stud in the Limousin became, and remains, the centre of Arab pure and cross-bred breeding.

Today, Anglo-Arabs are entered into the pure-bred register, if they have 50% Arab and 50% thoroughbred blood, or in the half-bred register, as long as they have more than 25% Arab blood.

The breed is so well established that the majority of modern Anglo-Arabs are the result of crossing Anglo-Arabs with Anglo-Arabs. They are fiery, attractive, horses and have been in demand as the mounts of the French cavalry, as racehorses in the South of France, as competition horses in jumping, eventing and dressage, as pleasure rides and as providers of a refining influence when crossed with the heavier breeds of the north.

The Arab strain in French horses helps to make them quick, handy and balanced, but rather more excitable and agile than the warmbloods of the Swedes and the Germans. It also tends to produce a more volatile temperament and great impulsion. This

suits French riders, who place greater emphasis on grace and
flamboyance than the highly disciplined Germans. The French
have produced a horse as suitable to their own character as the
Germans have to theirs.

Another characteristic of the French which emerges in their
horse breeding system is nationalism. Especially in recent years
they have restricted the use of foreign breeding stock. Imported
horses have to overcome almost insurmountable formalities
before they can obtain the necessary registration in the Selle
Français Stud Book. Even those imported for competitive
purposes have limited opportunities to participate. The reason
is simple. The French think that their blood is the best. They claim
they have enough variety of types, thoroughbred, trotter, Arab,
Anglo-Arab, warmbloods and work horses, to provide the blood
infusions needed to improve the strain.

But more important, the origins of French horses have been
controlled and documented, many since the time of the Sun
King, Louis XIV. Even the Anglo-Normans, the Charolais and
so on, have had their own stud books. The nationalistic French
want none of the more haphazardly bred English and Irish
horses. Also government doctrine had to be supported. The French
have become a horse exporting nation and do not want to turn
into an importing one. De Gaulle was not the only Frenchman
to believe that other countries, and their products, were distinctly
inferior. Horse breeders, too, are confident of the superiority of
their produce.

The project to produce a higher quality and larger number of
riding horses is directed by the government, and their involvement in breeding dates back to 1665 when the Service des Haras
was founded. This organisation now comes under the Ministry
of Agriculture, and has at its disposal part of the vast funds of
the Pari Mutuel (French Totalisator). Hence, the money earned
through horses goes back to help them again. To the French this
is quite logical and fair and they cannot understand why British
bookmakers should deprive the poor horses and their associates
of the money they were responsible for generating.

Chairman of the Service des Haras, which is one of the most
powerful equestrian organisations in the world, is Monsieur
Henry Blanc. A tall, thin, grey haired gentleman who is, like so

many Frenchmen, articulate and proud. He emanates confidence that the French are the best, and that he is running the most logical and efficient breeding organisation in the world. He has applied an intellectual approach to breeding and his aim is to have enough control to arrange, from government level, all the matings in the country.

Monsieur Blanc is assisted in his work by an officer at each of the 23 stallion depots. These officers are rarely horsey folk born and bred, but generally graduates in Agricultural Economics; the emphasis in France being to produce a rational system of breeding thought out by centralised organisers. All of these officers, together with lower grades of workers at the studs, take courses at the national school for studs at Le Pin. This school also runs courses for those who want to make horses their career.

The Service des Haras is not only a powerful organisation, but a wealthy one too and holds a near monopoly over breeding in France. With the exception of thoroughbreds they own most of the stallions in the country and they also compile and vet the applications for entry in the thoroughbred, Arab and Selle Français Stud Books. As a monopoly they take care to provide for all demands, having horses available to meet all equestrian needs. At each of the 23 depots, scattered throughout France, there are stallions suitable for production of horses for racing, competitions, pleasure, work and meat. Depot sizes vary, some only stand 40 horses, others as many as 200. In total the Service des Haras owns close to 2,000 stallions. Additionally, any privately owned stallions are subjected to the strict controls of the Service des Haras.

The valued qualities in French stallions are pedigree, conformation and the ability of their produce. The performance capabilities of the Selle Français is rarely tested, although the Anglo-Arab competes in races run in the south of France. There are no standard riding tests for 3-year-olds such as in Sweden, Germany, Denmark or Switzerland. It is interesting to note, however, that this point is under discussion and the French may soon follow the other European countries, and introduce their own performance tests for stallions.

Performance ability is already regarded as important for mares. Substantial subsidies are given to mares according to their successes in conformation, jumping, dressage and eventing competitions. As most of the owners of mares are small French farmers they rely on the subsidy to make breeding profitable. Consequently the Service des Haras as distributor of subsidies once again wields power.

The farmer can sell his produce profitably, the prices paid for young horses being at least as high as in other countries. The Service des Haras helps in this field too. They have a good supply of information about horses on the market and provide agents who will accompany potential buyers. There are about 500 registered professional dealers, including thoroughbred agents, but as there is less distinction between the various equestrian forms in France than Britain, the same person usually deals with all types of horse. Official assistance is redoubled if the possible purchaser comes from abroad, as the French export drive includes horses. They proudly publicise the fact that their horses have been exported to, and have won competitions in, Germany, Austria, Belgium, Brazil, Denmark, Spain, Britain, Italy, Morocco, Portugal and Switzerland.

The marketing of the Selle Français is now aided by an expansion of the auction system. Poitiers first arranged one in 1969. Within four years, prices and number of horses sold, doubled. Nowadays, there are three sales per year held at Poitiers. In May and October, for young Selle Français and Anglo-Arabs, and in November, for breeding and young stock. Vichy followed suit in 1971, and now holds sales after the international shows at Deauville and Vichy. It seems likely that in France, the warm-blood auctions will become as important and as respected a market as those held for thoroughbreds.

The Service des Haras has three research stations at which inquiries are made into the genetics, upbringing of stock, and the methods of mating. They also ensure their control over the purity of French blood by issuing all French pedigree documents, as well as export and import licences. Their work does not end with the actual breeding and selling, as they are also concerned about increasing the demand for their products, and in logical French fashion, they give considerable financial help to encourage riding in France. Competitors rely on the Service des Haras for a large proportion of their prize money, the equestrian societies for development programmes, tourists for riding holidays, and even the remount centres where horses are trained before being sent to the various clubs and schools. This dependence on government funds, the vastness of the amounts, makes private initiative insignificant, and has differentiated the French equestrian world from those in other western countries.

RIDING CLUBS AND CENTRES

The Service des Haras is having to expand the supply of Selle Français horses at the same time as improving its quality. The demand for them is rising fast because of the number of new riders. There was a sixfold increase over the last decade and there are now close to 200,000 French riders. The number of competitors authorised to ride has increased at an equally spectacular rate. In 1972 there were 7,057 of them and this was 12.96% (10% in Switzerland) higher than the previous year. From having been a sport confined to the rich and the army, riding has been democratised to encompass all classes. With this massive recruitment, which includes many lacking equestrian tradition, it has been difficult to maintain an adequate level of training. The provision of basic education for both horse and rider has been under strain.

As in other European countries the riding club is the base for equestrian activities. The clubs now bear the major responsibility for ensuring that the influx of riders is given adequate equestrian training. The number of permanent establishments attempting to cope more than doubled in the 1960s. There are now over 1,000 permanent equestrian establishments, encompassing a wide variety of types, more, in fact, than of any other country. This expansion, and provision of the best class of facilities, is largely due to the vast funds of the Pari Mutuel.

This money does not go only towards facilities for the serious rider and trainer. In France the more leisurely forms of riding are also promoted. Clubs for pleasure seekers and holiday makers (from home and abroad) are given encouragement and assistance by the government, who appear to want a healthy, active population, and regard riding as one of the best means of achieving this.

In order to entice the non-serious rider, and foreigners, out into the French countryside, clubs have been set up where equestrian activities may be the central theme, but where other attractions, such as luxurious hotels and a variety of sporting activities, are provided. It has meant that the clubs have become popular holiday and weekend locations, not only for equestrian enthusiasts, but also for people only remotely interested in riding.

In the French Ardennes there is the Posardes Estate. There, residents sleep in a comfortable rustic style clubhouse. They can take picnic excursions on horseback, or train seriously in an indoor school and an outdoor jumping arena. They can swim in a pool to cool off, and visitors can take French lessons for foreigners in their spare time. At Valency, in South Loire, they can stay in a castle, and apart from riding they can learn to drive carriages, and take part in amateur dramatics. At the Windmill of Villeneuve de Marc, between Lyon and Grenoble, both serious training and country excursions can be arranged. Swimming and trout fishing are amongst the non-equestrian diversions.

These establishments make use of historic buildings, but France can also boast of luxurious modern establishments. The most famous of these are run by the Club Mediterranean group. At the Nittel, Saint Guilian and Pompadour Mediterranean Clubs riding features and at Pompadour, in the middle of the Limousin country, close to the national stud, tuition is given to an advanced standard. At Pompadour, courses are held for jumping, eventing and dressage. The supervisor is well qualified. He is J. J. Guyon, who won an individual gold medal for France in the Mexico Olympics three-day event and his own education came largely from one of the world's greatest trainers, Jack le Goff. Those who come to the club for serious riding can find relaxing diversions. There is a swimming pool, a golf driving range, three tennis courts, carriages to drive, saunas, yoga classes, billiard tables, bridge games, concerts and a night club. Life at Pompadour must provide an exhausting but healthy holiday.

Riding clubs catering for the only faintly equine enthusiasts, by providing comfort and diversions, are an expanding feature in France. However there are the addicts who all too willingly submerge themselves in nothing but equestrian activities and these are catered for too. In 1975 the Federation recommended nearly 80 centres for their high-grade trainers and provision of regular advanced courses. Many of these schools specialise in particular fields and a few provide trained dressage horses, on which capable riders of all nationalities can learn advanced dressage. One of the most impressive of these schools is the Academie Equestre at Romilly-sur-Aigre, 100 miles south of Paris. There, fully trained Lipizzaner stallions are available for pupils to ride. The director is Monsieur Watier, the dressage champion of France in 1967 and 1968. He has created an exclusive establishment. Only two pupils are taken at any one time, and they are kept active. Each day they ride four horses, in four different lessons. They start with the *mise en selle* session, followed by two dressage lessons, and finally work from the ground, with a stallion using long reins and pillars. This programme aims to provide a comprehensive insight into the art of classical dressage. The individual nature of the lessons and the availability of schooled horses make it an important addition to equestrian establishments available in France.

The Academie Equestre is not the only one of its type in France. On the outskirts of Etampes, 55 miles south-west of Paris, is a club run by the Etampes Riding Society. They have 25 Portuguese and Lipizzaner stallions which are trained, and can be used by pupils to learn all levels of dressage movements.

For young dressage riders such schools are an excellent source of training, but many of the established stars use the L'Etrier in Paris. It is convenient for those who work in the capital, and the high standard of riders amongst the members means that the top trainers go there to give courses. These include the ex Chef of the Cadre Noir, St. André, Theoderescu and the Portuguese maestro, Oliveira. The L'Etrier Club is not made up entirely of competent horsement, for it is 'the' club of France, and has become a social centre for Parisiennes who think it smart to ride.

A school which should, however, surpass all others in regard to facilities is the national school of equitation. On the outskirts of Saumur, the home of the Cadre Noir, millions of francs are being spent on the most luxurious equestrian establishment yet built. It is planned to house 600 horses there, and for the top trainer in each of the three disciplines to bring on the most talented French riders.

Fontainebleau

In the past, Fontainebleau has been used as the national equestrian school, but lost this prestigious title in favour of Saumur. Even so, it remains famous for its picturesque and comprehensive equestrian facilities (this historic small town was the residence of the French kings before Versailles). Some are in the centre of town and others extend into the surrounding vast forests of pine and silver birch. Nothing should change, for the French are unlikely to chop down these historic trees which limit the town's growth and Fontainebleau should remain a little oasis, close to Paris.

The main part of the equestrian centre, is separated from the Palace by an acre or more of water which creates a stately and romantic background for the riders of Fontainebleau. On the edge of one side of the lake are two gardens. One garden is neat and carefully planned in geometric proportions. The other is much wilder and haphazard, with beds of mixed flowers. The former is called the French garden, and the latter, the English. It is a useful insight into how the French differentiate themselves from the British, and is a view which bears a level of truth when the two countries' horse breeding and training systems are compared.

The equestrian centre, which was originally built for the army, has stone barns, containing stalls and loose boxes along a central passage, with the most prized equine inmates living in a stable yard. There are sleeping quarters for the humans too, as well as offices, outdoor arenas, and three indoor schools. The most interesting of these was built in the time of Napoleon. The roof is the inverted hull of a ship. Apparently the Emperor wanted his carpenters to get some practice in constructing ships so that they could prepare a fleet for the proposed invasion of England.

It is the facilities in the encircling forest which make Fontainebleau such a great equestrian centre. It is not a dark foreboding forest, for the trees are far apart, and the trunks grow thin and high. Horse and rider can wend their way in between, and the light comes glimmering through. In the winter the smart citizens of Paris dress up to follow the hounds, chasing wild boar and deer, but at all times of the year serious minded competitors can find a vast range of cross-country fences to practise over. In one clearing there is a show jumping arena where European Championships have been held, and the French national show is staged each year. It is an intriguing and tricky arena for it is on undulating ground. It introduces fresh problems for the competitors as they have to take into account gradients as well as the size of, and distance between, fences. There are also formidable and unusual natural obstacles which include banks, ditches and walls. Jumping at Fontainebleau demands a wide range of skills from horse and rider.

These enviable facilities have been administered by a variety of authorities over the years. There have been a series of plans, as to how best to implement them. In the 1950s Fontainebleau became the Centre National des Sports Equestre and it was to be the world showpiece as a national school. Top horses were to be purchased by the Federation and top trainers were to school the top riders. Surprisingly, money plus facilities plus ideas did not produce success. The students of Fontainebleau won no great international honours. The Algerian war did have disturbing effects on the French at that time, but it seems the individuality and the temperamental nature of the riders and trainers were more serious and permanent handicaps. Since this rather disappointing venture, Fontainebleau has alternated between domination by the civilians to that of military. The present plans are for military occupancy and for Saumur to be the civilian centre.

Fontainebleau, despite constant changes of policy direction, has remained the venue of the national Championships in all three disciplines, the major school for training Grade I instructors (the monitors), and a centre for local competition riders. Many of the great show jumpers, such as Paul Rozier and Hugo Parot, live in this area, others bent on success take up residence close to these magnificent facilities. Shows varying from international to the easiest standard are staged throughout the year, and regular courses are held to prepare riders for competitions. Fontainebleau has become the most important equestrian area in France.

It is upon the training of instructors, rather than competitors, that Fontainebleau now concentrates. A five month long course is staged twice a year. These courses are open to foreigners and Belgians, English and even Germans are often among the students. Fontainebleau may not be as famous as Saumur but there are 120 horses available to pupils who can count on up to five rides a day. Also the instructors are civilians who tend to adopt an individual approach, different perhaps to that of the military at Saumur.

Saumur and the Cadre Noir

The French have style, tradition and taste; and the Cadre Noir an elite corps of the cavalry, display all these characteristics. They are based at the town of Saumur which lies between Angers and Tours, in countryside famous for its chateaux, some of which are magnificent, others are simple fortresses but all give evidence of the past strength and wealth of France.

Saumur was rather different from the surrounding towns, for it was a stronghold of Protestantism. Having to withstand the onslaughts of the more numerous Catholics, it became a fortified town. The chateau itself is easily defendable for it is on high ground, and overlooks precipitous slopes to the river Loire below. It now houses one of the best horse museums in the world, and the shops in the town are full of bric-a-brac, souvenirs, pictures and china adorned with horses. It is France's 'town of the horse'.

Saumur was chosen as a cavalry base in the eighteenth century. Legend has it that the dashing young cavalry officers were refused residence in Catholic towns because the citizens feared for the virtue of their womenfolk. It seems that the Protestants of Saumur were less fearful. Then, during the reign of Louis XVIII after the passing of Versailles as the Royal equestrian centre, the cavalry at Saumur founded the world famous Cadre Noir. They were formed as a corps of riding instructors, initially both civilians as well as members of the army were members. Indeed, the first écuyer en Chef (Commander) was a civilian.

The Cadre Noir takes its name from the colours of their distinguished uniform. They wear short black tunics, white buckskin breeches and, when in full dress, a black cocked hat. The buttons are gold, as are the epaulettes and the spurs of the officers. Members of the Cadre Noir catch the eye and are proudly conscious of it.

The corps is 24 strong and is divided as 12 officers, the écuyers and *sous écuyers*, and 12 non commissioned officers, the *maitres* and *sous maitres*. The division is so marked that it is very rare for a *maitre* to become an *écuyer*. Harbouring of traditions is an attractive feature of the Cadre Noir, but this particular one is subjected to considerable criticism from more egalitarian minded compatriots. In 1974, however, one tradition was changed and for the first time in more than 100 years civilians were allowed to join the corps. They were not the first to infiltrate the Cadre Noir this century for since 1969 civilians as well as the military have been accepted on courses. It will be interesting to see whether they bring in a little more of that *égalité*.

Dressage has been the most famous line of instruction with the Cadre Noir but, unlike other top schools, this is not due to specialisation. Both riders and horses are encouraged to partici-pate in racing, jumping, eventing and hunting, in addition to their dressage. Most members of the corps have tried their hands at all these disciplines. It is this stimulating variety which is one of the charms of Saumur, qualifying members to be able to meet the demands of many types of pupil, but perhaps accounting for a relative lack of competitive success.

The longest course at Saumur lasts for nine months and is aimed at preparing riders to become Grade II instructors. Like the corresponding course at Strömsholm in Sweden, it has become very international. The French still make up the majority of students, but others from Germany, Belgium, Holland, Japan and England often join this comprehensive training course. The other course for instructors is merely a refresher. Once a month, a two-week course is held for those who want to brush up their knowledge.

There is also a two-week dressage course on which the pupils from abroad often outnumber those from France. It has become, for the French, a prestige course enabling them to show off their Cadre Noir and their system of riding to the foreigners. For foreigners, it is an excellent opportunity to ride schooled horses, to receive knowledgable instruction and to obtain an insight into the French and their methods of riding.

The continuing support of the government for the expensive Cadre Noir is justified largely on prestige grounds. They believe this is gained by encouraging foreigners to appreciate their methods, and also through their famous dressage display – the Reprise of the Cadre Noir.

The Cadre Noir has appeared in displays the world over, demonstrating their version of High School, and when in France they give weekly displays at their manège in Saumur. The *Reprise* is divided into two contrasting sections of which the first is the *Reprise des Écuyers*. Light classical music strikes up to provide the background for the *Reprise* of the officers. They perform exercises hardly changed in more than a hundred years and which are straightforward dressage movements, for the aim is to perform as a team, to give a display of harmony amongst horses and riders so no one is permitted to outshine the others, and no spectacular movements are practised. The only person who is allowed to prove his superiority is the *écuyer en Chef*. He demonstrates his authority by making his horse perform the Spanish Walk and the passage whilst his follows do more ordinary walks and trots behind him. It is an elegant pleasing display; although lacking the spectacular effect of the Spanish Riding School's performances it has no equal as an exercise in discipline, the meaning of authority and comradeship.

The spectator's enjoyment is enhanced too by the contrasting nature of the second half of the performance. The music changes from romantic light classical, to a wilder strain and instead of the calm, well organised, entrance of the *écuyers*, into the arena dash 12 *maitres* known as the *Sauteurs*. Their horses are hefty with massive buttocks and are a sharp contrast to the elegant thorough-breds and Anglo-Arabs of the *écuyers*. The wild music stops suddenly, there is the bellowing roar of the *Capitaine* and the *maitres* form a line, or a circle, and make their mounts leap into the air to perform courbettes, croupades or cabrioles. The music starts again, as they return to the ground and they set off at a spanking pace until, again, a sudden silence signals more leaps. Originally these leaps were used in battle, but today they are performed in order to train the riders. During these ancient school jumps, the French riders lean right back and have no stirrups for support. It means they have to develop balance, and is a rather dramatic way of suppling their backs.

When the Cadre Noir is at Saumur the *Reprise* takes place every Friday in the oldest of the manèges. Here, there are stone galleries on three sides, and dignitaries and VIP's take the salute from the most ornate gallery. Outside there are no grass fields, for this is the centre of the town and horses have to cross roads and risk the speedy French traffic when returning to their stables.

There is another, more modern and less lavish, manège alongside, and across the road there are a few acres of sand divided into arenas by white railed fences. Around the perimeter and down the centre are avenues lined with trees. Show jumps are in some corners, dressage arenas in others. Everywhere during the day there are riders – leaping fences, galloping around the track, performing piaff and passage – and many of them use gadgets to establish mastery of their horse. Chambons, draw reins and the like are all used to achieve the popular French practice of 'showing the horse the ground' (i.e. lowering his head and neck).

On one side of this active area are the blacksmiths' forges, saddlery shops and more stables. On another, is a more distinguished looking building, which is an Academy for the army and recruits can often be seen running around amongst the horses on their get fit exercises. Saumur is still a major army base and, for the majority of those stationed there, the tank is much more important than the horse.

The equestrian centre has other facilities scattered in the outskirts of the town. There are the competition stables, where prized horses can look out on sandy grass areas used for lungeing and which contain banks and natural fences for instant practice. Frequent flurries of activity over these fences, and on the grass areas must keep the occupants of the stables well entertained.

A few hundred yards beyond the competition stables, the open land begins and here there are hillocks, banks, lakes, galloping tracks and a mass of natural obstacles. A few miles still further is the major training area for cross-country riders where the fences are bigger and more formidable. Situated well away from urban areas these grasslands are being built on to provide facilities for the French national school of equitation.

Until the completion of the arenas and schools the national school has made use of the Cadre Noir's facilities in Saumur. Working in such surroundings as these, it is difficult not to be affected by the curious aura of the Cadre Noir. For the corps members, and those connected with it, life is remote from the norm. They have established an enclave in this small town, where little is more important than getting their horses to perform extravagant movements, to run faster or to jump higher. The horse has become a wonderful means of showing off their ability, of making life stimulating and fun. Nor is it merely physical exercise for they have adopted an unusually intellectual approach. Riding gives them an opportunity that so many French relish to expound theories, to test new ideas and to criticise varying methods. There is a continuous exchange of views between comrades and it is easy to see how the French have developed equestrian theory over the years.

Clad in their distinguished uniforms, *maîtres* and *écuyers* can apply their own methods to train their horses. Some use draw reins, or chambons, and others look at these with disdain muttering 'gadgetry is the cause of France's poor results'. The French value individuality and variety is a key factor in the life of the Cadre Noir. Members race, jump, hunt and perform dressage and their horses receive the same treatment. On one occasion I was a little startled and fascinated by the variety of exercise given to a leading Reprise horse. Upon entering the manège the first exercise was piaff, but after half a dozen strides of this advanced movement the *écuyer* sent him forward into a canter on a loose rein with the horse's head nearly on the ground. To the onlooker's amazement he turned towards a formidable fence, and leapt it before going back into piaff. Such variety is the Cadre Noir's way of avoiding staleness overtaking their horses, and in producing that mainstay of French riding *l'impulsion*.

An even more risky incident occurred when a *Capitaine* decided to take his best young horse out hunting. It proved to be a quiet day and he became bored just standing by the covert, so he started to practise a little piaff. After a few minutes of this unusual exercise, a deer flashed by pursued by the hounds. The piaff must have developed the horse's power for they went like a bullet into the midst of the forest, making their way at an alarming rate through scrub, around trees and over ditches. The horse was no longer a subject for High School, but a means of transport across tricky terrain.

The abundant supply of horses, the thoroughly tested teaching methods, the allowance for individuality, and the facilities at Saumur make membership of the Cadre Noir a valuable starting point for any ambitious rider. Also it is Cadre Noir members, past and present, who dominate the French equestrian scene. Two past *écuyer en Chefs*, Colonel St. André and Colonel Margot train the best French dressage riders. Jack le Goff, once an *écuyer*, is trainer of the American three-day event team, and one of the most respected instructors in the world. Martin, a former *maitre*, is in charge of the other major French training centre at Fontaine-bleau. Of the present members the *écuyer en Chef*, Pierre Durand, is one of the most stylish and popular of the international jumpers, and Patrick Le Rolland is a top French dressage rider.

One of the best opportunities to study this stimulating and successful approach to riding is on the two-week long dressage course which is held once a month. The Cadre Noir's methods, ideas and basic formula, within which individualism is allowed, is presented to the foreigner proudly and with the obvious confidence that they are the best. As one officer said 'Le francais – c'est le classique pure, les autres sont classique mais dangereux'.

The French plan the fortnight carefully, information is handed out, although it is often altered and disregarded according to frequent changes in circumstances. The normal day starts with a session without stirrups (*mise en selle*) aimed at developing the correct seat. After this rather painful beginning, the pupils work indoors on older horses which have passed their days of brilliance but retain their ability to carry out advanced movements. An *écuyer* takes this lesson which is called *L'Ecole des Aides*, and entails advancing from basic aids to those used for piaff and passage by the end of the fortnight. In the afternoon there is a lecture on the theory of the work being done which provides an opportunity for the students to question the trainers. It is followed by another ride on trained horses when students can apply the movements developed in the morning's *L'Ecole des Aides*.

In every dressage school, a good seat is considered the pre-requisite of successful riding but this position differs between countries. The German likes to be straight upright and appears to be in much the same position as if he were standing up. The Swede tends towards a rounded stance, but the French push their loins forward and scoop their tail bone forwards and upwards.

The purpose of this is to have 'the horse in front of the leg', to be able to push with the seat bones and develop *l'impulsion*, the password to successful French riding.

Another feature of the French seat is the emphasis on suppleness. 'Souple, plus souple' is heard almost as frequently as 'L'impulsion, toujours l'impulsion'. Following from this idea of suppleness is the importance placed on leaving all pivot points free to absorb movement. The stirrup must not be further forward than the ball of the foot otherwise it restricts the mobility of the ankle. The knee must not be closed on the saddle (contrary to German and Viennese Schools) for the French believe that with free and relaxed knees the horse's movement is more easily absorbed.

Acquirement of a supple French seat, with the loins pushed well forward, is helped by the French saddle. The tree slopes sharply from a high cantle to the seat and the rider is pushed well forward. The saddle helps the student to adopt the French seat but there is a rather more dangerous and amusing method of ensuring that the lesson is properly understood. This is the *mise en selle* session when students, deprived of their stirrups, gallop up and down hills and over poles whilst adopting acrobatic positions on their horses.

In my case the *mise en selle* clan was led out on the first morning by a handsome young non commissioned officer. He thought life was wonderful and as we trotted through the streets of Saumur he would send his horse into passage if a pretty girl came in sight. We were told to push forward and down on our seat bones, to let our legs hang down and forward, to relax our ankles and keep our shoulders back. Then suddenly he turned off the road, disappearing down a precipitous sandy slope.

'Allez, allez' we heard from below and our school horses took charge pulling us down the hill. We found ourselves in a large sandy area crammed with drops, banks, fences, trees, ditches and crevices. Our instructor made his way at a trot and canter up and down hills and banks, around acute bends and over fences. It felt like being on a switchback at the fair.

Our gallant trainer kept turning to shout 'Les épaules en arrière', so we pushed our shoulders well back; but he was not satisfied, and stopped to demonstrate. We watched as he went over a fence with his shoulders nearly on the horse's hindquarters. That is how he developed his 'souple' back he told us, and that is how

PLATE 3
The Cadre Noir of Saumur perform a spectacular *croupade*.

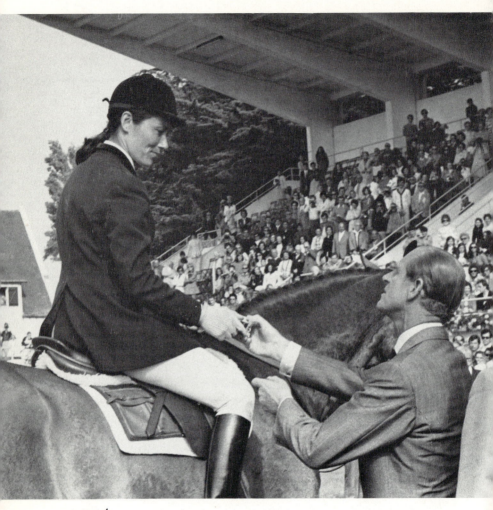

PLATE 4
Janou Tissot (*née* Lefebvre) the French ladies world champion in 1970
and 1974 receiving her trophy from Prince Philip.

every member of the Cadre Noir did it. We gaped in disbelief. It seemed a make or break method, but with the continuous cries of 'les épaules en arrière', we had to try. We leapt on to banks, over drop fences and set off at an uncontrollable canter with our 'épaules' getting further and further 'en arrière'!

After what seemed like a million years the *sous maitre* pulled back to the walk. His face was flushed red and he was beaming at the fun all these dashing activities had generated. He turned to us 'C'est amusant, n'est-ce pas?', but he saw six faces strained with the concentration of staying on and riders clutching sore behinds and backs. 'Maybe' a voice said 'it will be fun when we look back on it.' In fact when the stiffness began to wear off, and no one actually fell off, we did begin daring to relax and our back did become more 'souple', our seats more balanced, and we did have fun.

The most testing session came when France's only Olympic dressage rider at Munich, Patrick Le Rolland, took us. We had come to expect a few minutes walk, on leaving the stable and assumed that such a distinguished dressage rider would take us at an even more sedate pace. However, after a query as to our readiness, we were led off at a spanking canter along the sand, broken by an occasional trot when we hit a road. We careered along the tracks, around the stables for competition horses where D'Orgiex, the national show jumping trainer was lungeing a horse. Le Rolland's haughty expression broke into a wide grin 'A la chasse', he cried, and spurred his horse on faster. The grooms and others in the stables shouted encouragement and we wondered what was in store for us when we hit the jumping area. Our anxiety was not ill founded. Le Rolland disregarded the smaller obstacles and took on solid stone walls at a near gallop. We returned in equally flamboyant style and with great relief that we were still sitting in the saddle.

These risky sessions epitomised the spirit of Saumur. Neither horse nor rider are wrapped in cotton wool. Fun, dash, a little showing off, speed and impulsion are basic to that life. We were given, however, the occasional and less dramatic plain exercise session. We were told to bend and raise our knees so that the seat bones became the only connection with the saddle. We were told to swing our straight legs backwards and forwards, to hold on to the neck strap and lower our heads on to the trotting horse's hindquarters. For the French it was such fun to see us doing this that it made it amusing for us too, the laughter made one relax. It was a clever tactic.

There is another side to the French. They like to apply their intellect to everything, including riding. Consequently, at Saumur one gets this unusual combination of approach: on the one hand there is the premium on speed, dash and fun; on the other, the serious analysis of the horse's movements, the production of a wide variety of theories resulting in a complex and sometimes confusing approach to riding.

In most countries the horse is treated as a whole and is trained in the movements (shoulder-in, half-pass and so on) that are a test of its schooling. But not the French who consider the horse in parts and exercises are created to supple each of these. It is only in the final stages of training that the horse is treated as a whole and the movement itself attempted.

Again the French have analysed the action of the rider in minute detail, which makes for a complex theory. They have divided the rein aids into five different types which demands an intelligent and sensitive rider to be able to differentiate and make use of them. There is the simple open rein (changes direction) and the neck rein (moves the shoulder) both of which act on the forehand. However, the reins can also be used to have an opposing effect between the shoulders and hindquarters. These are called the reins of opposition. They consist of the direct rein of opposition which limits the action of the same shoulder and opposite hindquarters (turns the horse in the direction rein was applied); the neck rein of opposition, applied in front of the withers which moves the shoulders and hindquarters in different directions (turns the horse in the opposite direction to rein applied); and finally, the intermediary rein, applied behind the withers which has an effect between the direct rein of opposition and the neck rein of opposition (pushes the horse to the opposite side of the rein applied).

The leg aids, too, are finely differentiated. The position of the leg, the direction of its application and the manner of its application are considered and the results they can bring about are analysed.

Collection is also analysed in great depth, and the description of it is rather complex. In most countries it is described as simply getting the horse to take shorter and higher steps through the engagement and lowering of the hindquarters. But not the French, who consider it as the reduction in the size of the three angles, in the buttocks, between the second thigh and the thigh, and in the hock. The aim is to use exercises in order to supple up the horse and make it possible to reduce the size of these three angles. This establishes an interesting distinction between the French and the Germans. The Germans are practical, watching or feeling for the lowering of the hindquarters. The French are more intellectual, thinking about angles and creating exercises to make them smaller.

Not only do the French look upon collection from a rather different viewpoint, but they also place less emphasis upon obtaining it. For most extension is as important an aim, as is collection. This is partly due to circumstances, for the French use thoroughbreds and Arabs to whom collection is not so natural as it is for the more powerful German and Swedish horses. Consequently, at Saumur, the piaff and passage are not performed so often, nor, with exceptions, are they of such a high quality as in Germany.

The primary consideration of French riding is not collection, but impulsion. For this reason, the French are envious of the British who can gallop across country and who spend most of their time riding out of doors where impulsion is easier to develop. The French, like most European nations, ride for much of their time in indoor schools. They are very conscious of the ill effects this can have and how easily it destroys impulsion, so they have devised ways of avoiding this. They jump often, and they claim this forces the horse to collect himself before the fence. All but the very top dressage horses, when the risk is too great, have to face a wide variety of obstacles to make their life stimulating and exciting.

Any movement which shows the slightest tendency to inhibit impulsion is black listed and only used in exceptional circumstances. Turns on the forehand, travers, and half-halts are rarely seen, or talked about, at Saumur and lateral movements are never carried out at more than 40°. On the other hand every possible movement is performed at an extended pace. The emphasis in the half-pass is on 'ample' strides, and the rider aims for an extended stride in the two track work.

Impulsion is the central aim but there are others. In foundation work the first stage is to get the horse going forward after which 'la tension de la ligne dessus' can be established. The latter entails co-ordinating the various parts so that there is a line of feeling through the horse. The action of the hind legs is felt in the rider's hands, the sensation having passed from the hind leg through the body, neck and head to the mouth and back through the reins to the rider's hands. This should be an elastic tension and they believe it is best established by stretching the horse and so suppling him up. The French do this by 'showing the horse the ground'. With little or no contact on the inside rein the horses at Saumur spend many hours cantering around with their heads very close to the ground. Horses that do not do this naturally are quickly harnessed in chambons (reins running from the girth through the rings of the bit to an attachment on the bridle at the poll). With the horse's head near the ground and the rider pushing to make the hind legs come well underneath the muscles over the top of the back and the neck are extended to their maximum length. This supples them up and makes it possible to establish 'la tension'.

Having obtained 'la tension', then equilibrium should follow. This is established when the horse is balanced and can carry himself without relying on the strength of the rider to hold him up or push him on. The final aim of early training is to get the horse *mise en main*, 'on the bit'. This contrasts with Sweden where it is the primary aim of early training. Many Swedes I spoke to were suspicious of this stretching, or 'showing the horse the ground', as they thought it might put the horse on the forehand, and for them the central aim is, like the Germans, collection.

For the French, the basic requirements for a horse in any equestrian activity are: impulsion, 'tension', equilibrium, and 'on the bit'. With these achieved, specialised schooling can begin, but in all three disciplines the aims of suppleness, lightness, calmness and straightness dominate the method of work.

A feature of the development of dressage ability at Saumur, is the continuous use of exercises. A popular one is to ride a zig-zag serpentine, in which the angular turns are completed by the use of the rider's isolated leg turning the haunches around the shoulders, and so developing the lateral mobility of the hind-quarters; or by turning the shoulders around the haunches by use of neck rein and so improving the lateral mobility of the shoulders. Another is to develop the half-pass by leg yielding away from the wall and then returning in half-pass.

Whilst the Germans are content with trying to perfect the movement asked for in the test, the French, perhaps, find this boring and undemanding. They like to devise exercises to develop the muscles required; it gives them a chance to use their minds and means there is less danger of the horse anticipating.

THE TRAINERS

In the past the major source of trainers has been the army and in particular the Cadre Noir. Retired cavalry officers were able to give pupils a consistent framework to work from. Today, with the civilian domination of equestrian activities, a non-military education had to be organised. The French have general standards for instructors in every major sport and in each it is possible to obtain a state teaching diploma. The examinations that these teachers of football, athletics and riding take, are determined by the same formula and are all under the direction of the Ministry for Youth and Sport. There are written and oral examinations, tests in the art of teaching and in the practice of the sport.

In riding the holders of these diplomas are given titles. On passing the first examinations, they are entitled to be called monitors; after the second examination, an instructor and after passing the third, a professor. A monitor can qualify at the age of 18 having taken a five month long course at one of the designated schools, of which probably the most popular is Fontaine-bleau. To become an instructor, candidates must be 21 years of age, and have held the first diploma for at least a year. Most spend nine months at Saumur, the national school of equitation, before taking their examinations. To become a professor, candidates must be 25 years of age and have demonstrated their ability to carry out advanced medium dressage movements, to jump across country and to show jump. It is noteworthy that the oral discussion for this examination is orientated towards knowledge of classical methods, as established by the authors, Baucher, L'Hotte and Decarpentry, and in the manuals of Equitation and Jumping published by the Federation Français. The French riding professor needs more theoretical qualifications than his German counterpart, who is tested largely in the competitive sphere. The German has to train and produce horses for the arena and little value is attached to knowing how the classical masters of equitation said it should be done.

Colonel Margot

Although this French system of educating professional riders makes it possible for the civilian to acquire the highest qualifications, most of the leading trainers of France are members, or graduates of, the Cadre Noir. The pre-eminent members of the corps, the *écuyer en Chef*, has traditionally been the national dressage trainer. Colonel Margot who held the post after the Second World War was brought up in the days of Lesarge, France's greatest dressage champion of the twentieth century. During his era of glory, lightness, freedom and extravagance were generally thought more important than today's popular preference for precision. Colonel Margot today still supports the ideas that he learnt in his youth and follows them when teaching some of France's leading riders and at the occasional training session at the Cadre Noir.

Pierre Durand

Colonels St. André and Boisfleury succeeded Colonel Margot as *écuyer en Chefs*, and for both of them dressage was their speciality. In 1975 however Pierre Durand was appointed *écuyer en Chef* and his metier is show jumping. Although he is an all round horseman, he rode in the Rome Olympics as a member of the French three-day event team which won the bronze team medal, and performs in the dressage *Reprise*, it seems his great aim is to convert enthusiastic young members of the Cadre Noir into successful show jumpers.

In the past, riders from Saumur have starred in dressage and eventing, but show jumping has never borne such fruitful results. Pierre Durand sparkles with demonstrative French enthusiasm about changing this record. When he joined the corps in 1973, the riders practised a wide variety of styles. Although most adopted the speedy French approach, some went to the opposite extreme and tried to employ the precision orientated methods of the Schockemöhle school. Durand wants to establish a standard style that is a pleasure to watch. His aim has been to create a harmony between horse and rider, a living combination in which the rider is the brain and the horse executes the commands.

Durand has adopted intellectual type aims for his riding and has the great ambition to get them accepted generally. This aim is common to many of the French but is rarely achieved because of another characteristic – individualism. All the others have different standards that they want applied!

In Pierre Durand's view show jumping should conform to general riding rules. This means the horse must establish the requirements of the Cadre Noir – impulsion, 'tension', equilibrium and 'on the bit'. Then a course can be jumped with rhythm and balance making it less of an effort; the horse will have more energy remaining for the jump off and will have a longer competitive life. The problem with this idea is that style, the way the horse is going and the avoidance of interference can become ends in themselves and the matter of clearing the fence fades into the background. The American Olympic gold medal winner, Bill Steinkraus, is a great stylist too, but he claims he liked to think that his next meal depended on clearing the fence, and not how it should be done.

Pierre Durand has modified the traditional French style to enable him to cope with the large obstacles and the tricky distances between the fences. Traditionally, the aim in France has been to tackle the fences with (as always) great impulsion. This normally entailed great speed and little rein contact. Quick thinking French horses learnt to back off fences and look after themselves but when one fence follows closely on another the horse has little time to re-establish his equilibrium. Durand advocates constant contact on the reins and the maintenance of reasonable collection to overcome this problem.

At the same time Durand's horses are taught to look after themselves in their early years. At the novice stage they are jumped on a loose rein, and over lines of fences placed at set distances so as to make the horse more gymnastic. Durand is always creating new exercises over fences so that the horse will be made to think and to change his stride and use himself to clear the fence. The rider's purpose is to maintain balance and rhythm. An interesting point is that if the horse cannot work it out and arrives in the wrong place to take off, Durand allowed them to stop rather than hit the fence. Indeed at any time when the approach is not correct he prefers not to jump the obstacle. For him, harmony with the horse is more important than getting over an obstacle at all costs. There is a danger that his pupils will be riders with pleasing styles whom spectators want to watch, but from whom the competitive edge has been rasped.

Patrick Le Rolland

The most important non commissioned officer at Saumur is Patrick Le Rolland, who has worked his way to pre-eminence in the French dressage world. He represented France at the 1972 Olympic Games and has won the highest French placing in the 1973 and 1974 European and World Championships. His riding started at a small school, but it was after he joined the cavalry, and the Cadre Noir, that he rose to the forefront of the equestrian world. Normally he wears an aristocratic glazed expression that would reduce to timidity anyone it was directed towards. Then, suddenly, it breaks into a broad grin and the eyes twinkle. This contrast can be seen in his riding – an utterly determined approach to control the horse and a warm appreciation when it obeys.

Le Rolland takes classes and is especially able in the field of techniques. The half-pass he likes to develop out of a shoulder-in around the corner, and if equilibrium is lost in the half-pass then he suggests going straight back into the shoulder-in. On the other hand, if the pace was too rapid in the half-pass, then the inside rein should be locked and the outside rein used for checking. There is no doubt that inside his handsome head there is much knowledge. Pupils, however, have to accept his vociferous corrections of faults, but there is that great broad grin and twinkle when things go right. I felt that his division between right and wrong was deep and clear. Neither his horses, nor his pupils, could plead confusion of mind and direction; something which contrasted with so many of his countrymen.

FRANCE 41

Colonel St. André

Patrick Le Rolland was a protegé of one of the Cadre Noir's most respected *écuyer en Chefs*, Colonel St. André. The Colonel is short and thin, and appears to burn up an enormous quantity of energy. He has so many things he wants to do, and so many things he wants to say. He has a very French face, which seems to be made of rubber, forming a never ending variety of expressions. His eyebrows, wide and straight, run from a point high on the forehead to below the corners of his eyes. They are particularly expressive, not resting for a moment, appearing to move up and down with every word he speaks and every thought he thinks. With this mobile face it would be very difficult for him to disguise his thoughts, but he has no desire to do so. He loves talking and has strong views on all subjects. Naturally it is on riding, the theme of his life, that he expounds most wisely and enthusiastically.

Colonel St. André common to so many in France has a history in all types of riding. He used to race and has been an international show jumper, but it was in dressage that he made his greatest impact. His training was international, for he went to the Portuguese army school of Maifra after the Second World War. His 'Chefship' of the Cadre Noir started in 1964 and ran for 8 years. It was druing these years that he directed his interests towards dressage, but, like all Continentals, he had been trained in this discipline. It is, he pointed out, the discipline which is the basis of every equestrian activity; it is needed even to go cantering across a field. Colonel St. André added that if dressage was the basis of all riding, then there must be the most to it.

For St. André, dressage is not merely the most important equestrian activity, it is an art. For the riders of the calibre of Oliveira, Linsenhoff and Neckerman, their horses become a means of expression. He goes further than this. Dressage riders, he says, are the only artists who make their own tools. It takes years of modelling and training to achieve a means to their own self expression. The painter does not have to make this means of expression, his canvas and paints, nor the violinist his violin. This makes dressage a unique form of art.

The means of expression – the horse – should be large and eye catching, he says, have good paces, be a correct model or pattern and have a good character and temperament. The rider must learn to ride with a relaxed back and an open knee, for it is most important to have buffers to absorb the horse's movement. The legs must be well back and the contact with the horse very light.

Colonel St. André likes to break the horses in at 4 years, to play around with them for a year and, only after this, to start serious work. The aim of this initial training is to get the horse going forward and straight. When this has been achieved each part of the horse is exercised, according to the traditional French methods at the Cadre Noir.

For further training of horses, he said the most important points were to obtain impulsion and free paces. He told me that his greatest pleasure was to obtain an extended trot with rhythm, which was high and wide. This is the French school, the fun of impulsion and extension. Most of the riding is with the horse horizontal, and the lowering of the hindquarters to obtain collection for piaff and passage is left until the later stages.

He spoke of the major difference between the French and German schools. The latter are always aiming for collection and precision but, St. André thought, this all too often meant the sacrifice of art. With accuracy as the aim, it is rare to be able to ride with light contact and obtain free paces and according to St. André it only becomes an art when lightness is obtained.

Although confident that the French school was the most artistic, St. André is also aware that at present there are few good exponents of it. He is sad and frustrated that his country is not as able as in the past to show off her methods and dressage to the world. He blames the wide variety of doctrines within the country that do nothing but confuse the rider; a lack of discipline and the quality of the horse. He felt nationalism – the reluctance to import foreign and fresh blood – was making it difficult to improve the national breeds.

Colonel St. André's wealth of knowledge, his enthusiasm for dressage now benefit few. Since his retirement from the Cadre Noir he has given only occasional training sessions, to some of the best civilian riders, at the L'Etrier in Paris. They are fortunate for as only a great trainer can say 'There are no rules in dressage, it always depends on the circumstances'. He has no rigid system, just clear aims and a wide variety of methods that can be applied according to the varying circumstances.

Jack le Goff

The Cadre Noir's most successful previous member, Jack le Goff, has emigrated. The Americans have enticed him to their national three-day event centre. He has been there since 1970, training the event team and quickly proved his ability when the American team won the silver team medal at the Munich Olympics. He improved on this in 1974, when his riders won the team and individual World championship titles and in 1976 the individual and team Olympic titles. Now his services are sought world wide, and only Bertalan de Nemethy, his fellow national trainer (of show jumpers), can rival the popularity of his courses in England.

Le Goff's equestrian education has been comprehensive, and at one time he was a high class race rider. His father, a cavalry officer, was based in Berlin and there Le Goff learnt about German riding principles. His most formative years, however, were spent with the Cadre Noir where he was the *maitre d'Equitation* for 8 years.

Le Goff's most successful competitive sphere was eventing. He was the best French rider in both the Rome and Tokyo Olympics, and at the former made the greatest contribution towards the team bronze medal. However, it is as a trainer that he has produced even more impressive results. It was he who trained J. J. Guyon, who won an individual gold Olympic medal in 1968; it was he who trained the French junior European team champions in 1968 and 1969; it was he who trained the bronze team medal winners at the Punchestown World Championships. This is a formidable record and the Americans have shown great foresight in attracting him to their country.

Fortunately, the British too have recognised his ability. He has held an officially inspired course for young British stars. His success can be understood immediately he is seen training as he has two qualities which enable him to make best use of his broad base of knowledge – perception and dynamism. This tall burly figure stood in the centre of the arena at the British national equestrian centre issuing comment after comment. He became totally involved in the activities of his pupils. In the volatile French manner, he went so far as to cover his eyes in horror, or to leap up and down when something went wrong, but equally, was full of praise and delight when a movement was completed well. He created a lively, reactive atmosphere in which laughter and criticism were common. He had, too, vivid ways of describing faults: 'Put some petrol back in the tank', he shouted as a horse lost impulsion; and, 'That's not a sitting but a sleeping trot', he cried at another.

With him, again, the French maxim dominated – the importance of impulsion. That old adage, heard so often at Saumur, was used just as often by Le Goff, 'the horse must be in front of your leg'. Again, he stressed the importance of the seat in the production of this impulsion. Riders of horses with not enough petrol in their motors were told to massage with their seat.

Another maxim of Le Goff's was rhythm. He said that the rider cannot rely on natural rhythm, they must give it to the horse. 'They have to live with this rhythm, and become a pilot rather than a passenger.' He helped to emphasise this idea with his pupils in a rather spectacular fashion. He stood like a conductor, waving his hands, rocking back and forth with his body and singing, or almost shouting, 'rum te te tum, tum te te tum'. There could be no question of not understanding what this colourful trainer wanted.

In the actual work that Le Goff asked his pupils to do, in keeping with the French, he used exercises out of which to develop the movements. He used voltes before going into shoulder-in, or canter, so that the horse was correctly positioned. The collected canter he developed by gradually reducing the size of the circle so that the horse had to slow down and engage his hindquarters if he was to turn in the reduced area.

In jumping he again used exercises. This time over grids, lines of obstacles placed at set distances. The object of this was to train the horse to co-ordinate and improve jumping ability and style. With set distances, the rider did not need to interfere and place the horse, and the distances could then be altered so that the horse took long strides or short ones, learning to jump off both, and to alter the length for himself. This improved his gymnastic ability. Le Goff, like Durand, said that by developing a style with a calm approach to fences the horse will use less energy, and this is all important both in jump offs and in retaining strength for three-day events.

Although at single and larger fences he maintained the rider could place the horse, during these gymnastic exercises the sole aim was to be in harmony with the horse. For this to be achieved, the rider had to determine the direction so that the horse was straight at the fence; he must control the speed so that it was appropriate for that particular obstacle; he should also keep the horse balanced, in rhythm, and maintain impulsion. These views reflect the influence not only of the Cadre Noir, but also of the world's most famous show jumping trainer, Bertalan de Nemethy, who works with Le Goff in America.

Martin

One former *sous maitre* from the Cadre Noir who benefited from Le Goff's training was Martin who is now the chief instructor at Fontainebleau. During his 5 years at Saumur he was one of their star competitors in eventing, coming fourth in the individual placings at the 1970 World championships at Punchestown (Ireland). Martin is another burly figure, with jet black hair. He emanates exuberance and energy, seldom standing still and reinforcing his instructions with gestures, jokes and laughter. He is full of ideas but dispirited because he cannot achieve enough of them. He is sad because he thinks there has been a wastage of horses, riders and money in French equestrian circles.

He says the major problem is that riders are not given enough opportunity to learn the elementary basic principles. It is only when these have been established that consistent and successful riding is possible. At present too many are unaware of the long term handicap of taking short cuts, and the authorities do not help for they spend too much energy and money on the show-pieces of the nation (prize money, buildings and shows) rather than in teaching young riders about this.

As the nation's premier trainer of the first level of instructors – the monitors – Martin would like to see improvements in the methods of training instructors, with the aim of establishing more uniform methods instead of the present diversity with the consequent wastage and conflict.

At Fontainebleau Martin has had an opportunity to establish some of his ideas, through his training of the monitors and he hopes to convince an increasing number of these future trainers of the importance of basic groundwork. For students, basic knowledge starts with 'the seat', and until this has been established it is impossible to apply aids correctly and consistently. However successful or grand his pupils may be, they still have to establish this, but then their prospects are good as there are over 120 horses at their disposal. Martin uses his own ability as a rider to get the horses going *juste* spending as much time riding as instructing. He thinks a horse going *juste* is essential for his pupils who must get the correct feel. It is only through feel that a pupil can know what to aim for in training horses and riders in the future. Martin also added that for instructors, knowing the correct feel is not enough; they must be able to analyse it and describe it to other people.

Martin's students are fortunate in having horses to ride which enable them to acquire feel and also that their professor encourages competitive riding. He claims that as present day equitation is based on competition, instructors must go into competitions to obtain a thorough understanding of the circumstances which will enable them to help their pupils. At Fontainebleau 60 of the better horses are reserved for competitive work.

Guy Lefrant

Martin is not the only trainer at Fontainebleau. One of the most successful all round competitors in France is in charge of the event riders who train there. His name is Guy Lefrant, and he has won Olympic medals in both show jumping and eventing. In 1952 he won the individual silver medal for eventing and in 1960 the team bronze. Then in 1964 he switched to the show jumping team and with d'Oriola and Janou Lefebvre won the silver team medal. This unique competitive knowledge is now at the disposal of the French event riders.

Jean d'Orgiex

Perhaps the most influential trainer in France is one of the few who has not had a Cadre Noir education. He is Jean d'Orgiex and is the national show jumping trainer at the Ecole National d'Equitation at Saumur. His character is hardly one which would be receptive to army discipline, for he has led the life of an adventurer. Under his father's tuition he became the leading

French show jumper after the Second World War, winning a bronze individual medal at London in 1948. When, in the early 1950s, his show jumping successes became less numerous he turned to other excitements. He spent some time in the theatre, then became an aerobatic pilot and finally spent 10 years safari hunting in Africa.

Jean d'Orgiex is an imposing person whose huge frame, air of authority, and total confidence dominate wherever, or whoever, he is with. He has the French dynamism, enthusiasm and abounds with theories and ideas. On the subject of horses he has presented his views in three published works. These were written in the 1950s and he admits today that he has had to make some adjustments to modern conditions. Now his aim, like so many others, is to get a uniform set of principles for show jumping established throughout France.

The first principle d'Orgiex advocates is to develop a natural equilibrium for the horse. The young animal must learn to carry himself without support on the flat and over fences. The rider must use a loose rein and not interfere at all. It is a development of Le Goff's approach who teaches his horses to look after themselves down lines of fences. D'Orgiex wants them to do it over single fences too, which makes an even sharper contrast with German methods. There the horse is typically taught (mainly with draw reins) immediate and total obedience to the rider. The equilibrium is imposed, whereas d'Orgiex wants a natural one.

Once natural equilibrium is established, d'Orgiex aims to make the horse totally obedient to the rider. For him, in similar fashion to Paul Weier in Switzerland, the higher the standard of jumping the more control the rider should exercise. In the final stages of jumping d'Orgiex demands total obedience from the horse.

This theory of d'Orgiex's is at variance with the general French style of jumping. At present, especially as most of the top riders are former steeplechase riders, and combined with the national reverence for impulsion, fences are tackled at great speed. Riders tend to set off at a dashing pace, rarely trying to adjust the stride, but allow their horses to steady up and back off the fence. This is in contrast to the traditional English method, where the fences are approached with collection and the rider waits until a stride is seen, before increasing the pace into the fence.

D'Orgiex proposes to teach advanced French riders this English approach. He hopes to get countrywide acceptance of his principles by distributing a series of films illustrating his methods. Also he will choose the most promising young riders between 17 and 20 years of age, and bring them to Saumur for courses. At present d'Orgiex has four young riders under him at Saumur. He is also training young horses which he will pass on to favoured pupils. He accepts, however, that there are talented riders in France who are too well established to be moulded into his ways. He does not try to convert them, but in his capacity as *chef d'equipe* on international tours, he merely says when a fault has been made and will suggest a correction within their style of riding.

D'Orgiex is confident that if his methods are adopted the French will offer a more serious challenge to the Germans on the international jumping circuit. To make this an even greater certainty he would also like to see a change in the nature of the courses. The Germans, he said, are successful because with their big, brave horses they can tackle the massive fences that are so fashionable today. At the same time the upright fences which are not so imposing and require a careful horse, accurately placed for take off, are less common. The latter are the fences d'Orgiex feels are the better test of the jumping ability of both horse and rider. They demand a more collected horse, and a rider who can place his horse accurately and with balance. It will be interesting to see how great an impact d'Orgiex and his ideas will have, both in France and the rest of the world.

ADMINISTRATION AND COMPETITION

The directors of French equestrian activities are a formidable team. The Ministers of Agriculture, Sport, Youth, Tourism, Defence, Education, Environment and Economics sit on the Inter-ministerial Equitation Committee. They have ultimate control, although executive power lies with the Council for Equitation. Eight government ministers sit on the Council together with equestrian specialists and the heads of the major equestrian associations. Under them in each of the 21 regions are similarly constituted Conseils. These are officially in charge of equestrian activities on a local basis, but they have to vie for authority with a number of societies, all with their own sphere of influence and clinging on to their bit of power. There are over 800 associations dealing with some aspect of riding, all of a non-profit making nature. It seems that if a particular problem is not dealt with satisfactorily, another association springs up to try.

The budget for the development of equestrian activities is enormous, and comes from the funds of racing – the Pari Mutuel. In the 1970s more than a million pounds have been allocated annually to non-racing, equestrian activities. It is enough to make the mouths of riders in other countries, water. The chief benefactors include the shows which rely on these funds for their prize money, the international teams, pupils and instructors, schools for their buildings and equipment, the equestrian tourist association and the Ecole National d'Equitation.

The funds are distributed through a number of associations whose functions can overlap. These include the Association for Tourist Equitation, the French Equine Society and the Association for Professionals in Equestrianism. The most famous and powerful, however, is the French Federation of Equestrian Sports. It controls all aspects of competitive riding and is responsible for rules, distribution of prize money, sending teams abroad and the purchase of horses for their Olympic riders.

In 1973, 90,000 members elected Dr. Pouret to be President of the French Federation. He is a retired veterinary surgeon, stud farm owner and trilinguist and is determined that the vast funds available should be used towards gaining more constructive results in the future. He believes this will mean preventing the multiplicity of ideas and associations, merging various interests, and ending the present divisions and rivalries. While outsiders glow with envy at the size of the sums being distributed, Dr. Pouret saw disadvantages in this. Success, he believes, is often best achieved through private enterprise. State organisation tends to deaden enthusiasm and stifle competition. Equestrianism in France could be in danger of this due to the involvement of the government, and the vast sums which they distribute. This is what he hopes to change.

The Société Hippique Français is an organisation started by retired army officers in 1886. It organises events aided by funds received from the Service des Haras. These funds are distributed on the understanding that the money helps to promote the development of the French horse. With this money the society finances national, but not international events. It also gives assistance towards the running of equestrian establishments. A subsidy of up to 50% is given towards the building of indoor riding schools and stables and some £3,000,000 was paid out in the 1960s in this way, aiding the increase in the number of equestrian establishments to over 1,000. The Société Hippique also helps towards the running costs of these equestrian centres, consequently, its financial help has been a major factor in turning riding into a sport enjoyed by all classes and not just the rich.

In this country of multifarious associations, there is also one for the competitors known as Le Club des Habits Rouge. It was formed to ensure that competitors' interests were not disregarded and to promote in the competitors themselves a sporting approach.

Competing in France is a profitable business. The shows do not have to depend on courting sponsors, getting television rights, or attracting large crowds in order to provide high prize money to the victors. The funds of the Pari Mutuel subsidises French prize money which, as for their racing, is as high as in any other country. Over 80% of all prize money (6,384,663 francs in 1973) is obtained from the Pari Mutuel funds.

Between March and November there are numerous opportunities to compete for this high prize money as there are nearly 500 shows, double that of the early 1960s. The eventing world has not been neglected and, unlike England, there is no mid-summer break. One, two and three-day events take place continuously from March to October and number well over 100. It is in dressage, however, that there has been the biggest increase in the number of competitions. They quadrupled in the 1960s and now they approach 100.

In French fashion, the rules concerning competitions are numerous and complicated. Riders in jumping competitions are separated into four categories. Category 1 covers international riders. Then there are four grades of classes A, B, C, D and category 1 riders can have three horses in an A class, but cannot ride horses in C or D. Category 2 riders can only ride horses that have won more than 10,000 francs in A competitions. Categories 3 and 4 cannot go in A, and categories 2 and 3 cannot go in D. That is just one group of competitions, the French are determined to keep their citizens' minds working!

In addition, there are the simpler, English, type categories dependent on the amount the horse has won and, finally, there is the most controversial group of all, the Epreves d'Elevage. These are competitions confined to horses from one age group, for 4, 5 and 6-year-olds entered in the stud book Selle Français. It means that to gain the benefit of low courses, horses must start competing at 4, otherwise they have to face the larger courses for 5-year-olds. This inducement to break horses in early and compete with them, is considered by many a reason for so many damaged horses.

The number of riders who have to work out these complicated rules is increasing rapidly. In the 1960s the number of show jumpers quadrupled, eventers tripled and dressage riders rose eight times.

The riders of show jumpers, as in other successful nations, are usually full-time. As yet they are still tagged as amateurs, but their official occupations take up little of their time. The prices of horses are as high as anywhere which encourages similar arrangements to those in Switzerland and Germany. Many top riders have large stables in which they, personally, own only young horses. These they usually sell profitably, often to a rich owner who only wants the fun and prestige of having a horse. Consequently the horse stays in the yard.

Coming into this category is Hugo Parot, a former steeplechase jockey, who is one of the comedians of show jumping. His showmanship and ability have given much to the sport. Another former jockey is Marcel Rozier. His fluent style provides an attractive picture when competing. His successes include membership of the silver medal winning team in the 1968 Olympics, and both these race riders were members of the gold medal winning team at the 1976 Olympics.

The most attractive French rider is the Saigon born Janou Lefebvre, now married to the business tycoon, M. Tissot. This petite, dark, pretty rider has been winning international events since she was seventeen. At that age, in 1961, she beat all her elders to win the French championship. Then she became the youngest rider in the 1964 Tokyo Olympics and helped to win the team silver medal there and again in 1968. In 1970 she became the ladies World champion and retained the title in 1974.

France has many excellent riders, but she has one who is head and shoulders above everyone else. He is Pierre Jonqueres d'Oriola. Born in 1920 he has gained every top show jumping honour to be won. This flamboyant dashing showman who farmed a large estate in the Pyrenees burst upon the international scene in 1947. In London that year he galloped around the King George V course at the Royal International Horse Show to take the trophy from the rather sedate, precision conscious, British riders. He stimulated a re-appraisal of British riding, especially when he confirmed the success of this flowing speedy style by winning the individual Olympic gold medal at Helsinki in 1952. His partner in this great victory was Ali Baba, a tiny Anglo-Arab former army horse, that had originally been used for polo.

His successes were not restricted to one horse, for he won intercontinental championships, world championships, national championships, all with different partners. His genius was confirmed, when on a horse in its first year of international competitions – Lutteur B – he claimed his second individual Olympic gold medal. He is the only person to have won two individual Olympic equestrian medals for show jumping. It is a formidable record and France recognised their champion when they gave him the Legion d'honneur (Cavalier).

It is in dressage that there has been the biggest boom in the number of French competitors. From amongst them international stars are beginning to emerge. Patrick Le Rolland, whom I mentioned earlier, has earned for himself high placings in continental championships. It has been, however, Mademoiselle Dominique d'Esmée who has been winning the leading prizes since 1974. She has the distinction of having won both the three-day event and the dressage French national championships. Today she concentrates on dressage and she is noted for tests which are full of gaiety, impulsion and activity. This approach has won for her the 1975 international Grand Prix competitions at both Fontainebleau and Goodwood. On both occasions she beat leading (if not the top) German riders and her success was greeted with enthusiasm for it proved that the flowing, fluent and more artistic riding of the French can beat the precise accurate methods practised by the majority of winners in the 1960s and the early 1970s.

It is to be hoped that these signs of a revival in French dressage can be maintained and the nation to whom the whole world is in debt for the development of equestrian theory can produce more international riders worthy of their great French heritage.

CHAPTER TWO

WEST GERMANY

THE ability to plan for success, combined with the determination, discipline and wealth to put the plans into effect, has made West Germany today's dominant equestrian power. She has won more Olympic, World and European medals in equestrian events than any other country in the world.

Like Britain, Germany does not rely on a small group of riders for her achievements. The base of her talent is broad and new stars in all three Olympic disciplines (show jumping, eventing and dressage) are continually appearing. From club to Olympic level, the Germans can field more riders in jumping and eventing competitions than any other country, except possibly Britain. In dressage they are unchallenged for the quality and quantity of their riders.

The remarkable success of the Germans must be due in some part to the natural talents of their riders, but in addition they have planned and developed a system which ensures that these talents are made full use of. In every aspect of riding the training and facilities are more comprehensive than those of other countries.

Their horses have been systematically bred so as to produce the best types for competitions. Their riders can have the best possible instruction as the German equestrian education system produces the largest number and the highest standard of trainers in the world. Their competitors can go to shows all the year round and have the additional incentive of high prize money.

These provisions are made full use of for it is in the nature of the German to want to succeed and they seem able to adopt a single minded approach in order to do so. The authorities naturally encourage this, handing out medals as a further incentive in the riders' quest for glory. Bronze is given for lowly achievements, silver for the best at national level, and gold for international successes. A Riders Cross is the ultimate honour which is given to those who have helped the sport in an exceptional way.

Germany has a clearly defined ladder for ambitious riders. Every assistance is given to climb it and every possible reward for those who do. It is a system which might well be the envy of many, but which more individualistic, less disciplined and poorer nations find difficult to adopt.

THE HORSE

Germany was one of the first to specifically set out to breed a riding horse, the warmblood. They approached the subject in the same way as did the British for the thoroughbred. The type required was analysed and specified. Stamina was thought unimportant, for hunting was rare. Speed was disregarded and thoroughbred breeding left to an entirely separate organisation (unlike France and Sweden). What was wanted from the horses in Germany was power, good temperament and extravagant movement. Matings were arranged to achieve these aims.

Riding horses, instead of being cast offs from the racecourse, or the result of a haphazard mating between the farmer's old mare and the local stallions, were systematically bred. Pedigrees of German warmblood horses are just as comprehensive, and are of equal importance, as are those for thoroughbreds in Britain.

This planned, calculated, breeding has been carried out at a regional level. Like France, each area produced their own breed of horse. However, three of the warmblood breeds emerged as the most successful and distinctive types. These were the Trakehner, Holstein and Hanoverian.

The Trakehner

The Trakehner (sometimes called the East Prussian) typically has flat hindquarters, a highly placed tail and a crest near the poll. They have a very colourful history. Their state stud was founded in 1732 by Frederick I (father of Frederick the Great). Thoroughbred and Oriental horses were crossed with the local work horses. the Schweiken, to provide stock and revenue for the royal stable.

The Kaiser was responsible for one of the most important

developments in the evolution of the modern Trakehner. He wanted a lighter, more flexible, horse for his troops. Arab blood was used to make the Trakehner one of the first breeds with the characteristics of today's warmbloods. The Kaiser wanted also a uniform bodyguard so through careful planning, black was made the predominant colour in the Trakehner.

This breeding was done at the Royal stud of Trakehnen, which now lies in East Germany close to Olstzyn in Poland. The stud was surrounded by 34,000 acres of marshy ground, rich in the lime and phosphorus which suits the rearing of horses. The breed expanded, and by 1939 there were 25,000 registered brood mares in the hands of 15,000 breeders. Every farmer and small-holder in the area was a breeder and it became known as a paradise for horses.

Unfortunately it was also a disputed area between east and west. On five occasions war had forced the evacuation of the stud. But the most disastrous blow came in the winter of 1944/45. With the Russians' arrival imminent, a small group of local breeders decided to flee to the west. They collected a few of the best stallions and 700 mares which were mostly in foal. The refugees harnessed some of the horses into carts enabling themselves and their belongings to be carried to the safety of West Germany. The horses on this trek across Germany through the winter of 1944 formed the nucleus of today's Trakehner of West Germany.

These mares and stallions were sold all over Germany. A Trakehner association was formed, however, to control breeding and which set up a stud at Rantzau in Schleswig Holstein. The surrounding area now contains large numbers of Trakehners and the facilities at the town of Neumünster are used both for auctions and the showing of Trakehners.

The Holstein

Like the Trakehner, the Holstein breed was developed in fertile marshland, but in a less vulnerable area. It was on the banks of the Elbe in Schleswig Holstein that the farmers and royalty took to breeding these rather high actioned horses with convex heads.

The type was derived from the importation of Neapolitan and Spanish blood, as far back as the thirteenth century. However, it was the establishment of the Royal Stud at Esserom in 1680 that marked the great expansion of the breed. In the ensuing years there was an important interchange of blood between Germany and England, with Cleveland Bays and thoroughbreds helping to improve the Holstein strain. Again, in the last fifteen years, carefully selected thoroughbred blood has been introduced to change the Holstein from a coach and artillery horse into a show ring type.

It has been a highly successful evolution. One of the most famous show jumpers of all times – Fritz Thiedemann's Meteor (two gold and one bronze Olympic medals to his credit) was a Holstein, and so were Fritz Ligges' Robin and Hans Winkler's Romanus and Torphy. In dressage too Holsteins have shone. Josef Neckermann's Venetia and Antoinette were both Holstein.

Elmshorn is now the centre for Holstein administration and activities. A vast riding school with a selection of outdoor arenas, stables and an indoor school, is the venue for sales of, and head-quarters for, this famous breed.

A privately run Holstein Association controls the activities of the breed. They took over this responsibility from the state government of Schleswig Holstein and now own stallions which stand on private farms.

The Hanoverian

In the modern competition world it is the Hanoverian which has become the most famous of the German warmbloods. The success of this breed seems to be their ability to adapt to the needs of the time. They have evolved from the heavy Great War Horse of the Middle Ages into the elegant competition horse of today.

The first stage of this evolution began when the introduction of gunpowder led to the need for a more mobile cavalry. During the seventeenth century the Hanoverian was fined down into a cavalry mount. The next great demand was for carriage horses and again the Hanoverian was adapted. It was royalty who played a major part in this development, especially after England acquired their Hanoverian king. This resulted in an interchange of equine as well as human blood. English thoroughbreds and Hanoverians found themselves exchanging homes resulting in a more refined Hanoverian. Another important step was taken in 1735, when

George II of England founded the famous stud of Celle. It remains today the state stud for the Hanoverian breed.

The Hanoverian proved to be one of Europe's most fashionable breeds of carriage horses, and by the twentieth century was also popular as an artillery horse for the German army. After the Second World War, however, few horses were needed for either of these occupations, the demand being for a riding horse. Once again, the Hanoverian needed to be adapted. From a rather hefty horse he had to be fined down and at the same time the straight shoulder and common head had to be eradicated.

Trakehner, Arab and thoroughbred blood was used to do this. The result today is a very distinguished looking horse, close to thoroughbred in type, yet retaining the movement and temperament of the old fashioned carriage horse. These Hanoverians have won many honours. In the 1972 Olympics, 31 Hanoverians carried riders from eight different nations, winning two gold medals, one silver and one bronze. However, their greatest achievement was in 1974, the World Championship year, when they won two of the individual titles. Mehmed was World Dressage Champion and Simona World Show Jumping Champion.

The successes of the breed stem from the work of the Hanoverian Society which must be the most adventurous, industrious and meticulous of breeders' associations in Germany. Over 7,000 mares are registered in their stud book, and each of these has been examined for type, conformation and paces before being entered. Some are rejected after an inspection at three years of age, some are put in the appendix, the better ones in the stud book, and only the very best in the full stud book. The greatest honour of all is to be given a State Premium – an award for the top performers in ridden tests.

The Hanoverian Warmblood Association stallion show is one of the features of the German equestrian year. This show is held in September, at Celle, the breed's 250-year-old stud, north of Hanover. The performers are the two hundred or so stallions, all of whom have passed rigorous selection tests. The public can see for themselves the high standard of performance demanded of the Hanoverian stallion before being allowed to have progeny. The 3-year-olds carry out dressage and jumping tests and the older horses show off circus like tricks, lying down and standing on their hind legs upon a word of command. The climax is a chariot race for the stallions, who pull their carts at breakneck speeds around a small dirt track. It is a remarkable exhibition which cannot fail to convince spectators that these Hanoverians possess the three features of German warmbloods, power, temperament and movement.

The variety of breeds

Although the Trakehner, the Holstein and the Hanoverian are the best known breeds in Germany, other areas have produced their own equine race.

Next in quantity to the Hanoverian, and very similar to them, is the Westfalian. Their stallion depot was established in 1826 at Warendorf.

The Oldenburger is also bred in large numbers. It is a rather heavy horse, often as high as 17 hands and which has become popular as a driving horse. The Oldenburger takes its name from the town, east of Bremen, which is the centre of the area where breeding takes place.

Other well-known breeds are the Württemberg and Bavarian in the south; the Hessan, Rheinlander and Rheinland Pfalz from around the Rhine. Yet none of the German warmbloods are pure-breds, as the only stipulations for registration in each stud book are that the horse was born in the area of the breed; that it has an accredited pedigree; and that it has passed its breed association examination. Consequently the pedigrees of German horses contain ancestors from a variety of breeds. The aim of the German breeders has been, and remains, to produce the best type of horse and not to breed pure-breds. A Hanoverian with nothing but Hanoverian ancestors would be difficult, if not impossible, to find.

The result of this approach is that much crossbreeding takes place and the various breeds of warmbloods in Germany are becoming increasingly similar. The natural development would be for all to amalgamate (as in France), to establish the German warmblood. The obstacle, up to now, has been regional pride, as there has been a tradition for states to vie with each other to produce the most successful breed in their area. The respective governments have actively promoted, assisted and directed the breed of their area. Today, however, the national government is reducing the effects of this rivalry by introducing general rules about breeding, to which all breed associations must conform. Also, leading officials are known to favour the merging of breeds so that the advent of the German Riding Horse (similar to the Celle Français) seems near at hand.

The selection of stallions

National, as opposed to state, regulations were established after the Second World War, when it became law that no stallion could be bred from unless licensed. These licences are only given to stallions whose pedigrees have been validated by their breed society, whose dam and sire have proved their performance ability, and who have themselves been examined by a state licensing committee. The latter only give licences to stallions who show the characteristics of their breed, and who have such excellent conformation and paces that their progeny is likely to raise the standard of the breed.

In addition, since 1975, it has been compulsory for all licensed stallions to spend 100 days being trained for riding and driving and to take, and pass, performance tests. These consist of dressage, show jumping and cross-country tests and a timed gallop upon completion of this last phase. Although the actual performance is the most important consideration, marks are also given for the manner in which the test is performed. Consequently, style, temperament, character, willingness to work, constitution and even fodder conversion play a part in the final result. The results are recorded and the owners of mares can then consider the performance figures when choosing a stallion.

Some breed associations lay down even stricter tests than these national obligations. The Hanoverian Society, for example, do not allow any stallions bought by the Celle state stud to serve mares as three-year-olds. Instead, they are trained for the entire spring and summer. The training takes place amidst luxurious facilities, in an equestrian centre, Adelheidsdorf, which is close to Celle. The centre was built by the Hanoverian Association and opened in 1975. There are 100 stables, with every possible mechanical device to cut down labour costs, outdoor and indoor schools and a cross-country course for training. The young Trakehners, Holsteins, Rheinlanders and Hessans also use these elaborate facilities to complete their obligatory 100 days of training.

It seems that the majority of young warmblood stallions in Germany will now pass through Adelheidsdorf, but only the very best reach this stage. There is a rigorous selection process which sifts through the 2-year-old entires. The first stage for most of the German breed associations is the appointment of a commission to examine the young stallions with good pedigrees. In 1975 the Hanoverian Society selected 80 of the 324 stallions they inspected, and these were allowed to enter the autumn Hengstkörung (stallion show and market).

Although most of the breeds organise a Hengstkörung, the Hanoverians' is the most famous, and international. It takes place at Verden, a small town situated between Celle and Bremen which is known as the Town of the Horse. There is a horse museum, a racetrack, show jumping arenas and their like which keep its many equine visitors amused.

The Hengstkörung is held at the Hannoversche Reit und Fahrschule where the activities are alternated between a vast indoor school and an outdoor arena. During the first two days of the Hengstkörung the young stallions are shown off to a panel of eminent equestrians – the commission of the Hanoverian Society. These gentlemen have to choose the ten horses they want to buy for the Hanoverian state stud of Celle, and they classify all the stallions according to their manners, conformation and paces. Judgements are based on watching each 2½-year-old entire being stood up, walked and trotted around the arena. Owners and friends crack whips in the centre to encourage these youngsters to show their presence and paces to their best advantage.

Amongst the audience are buyers from German state and private studs, and others from Switzerland, Sweden, Canada, Austria, Denmark, Belgium, Holland and, occasionally, Britain and America. The Hanoverian blood is considered one of the best means of injecting substance, temperament and paces into other breeds. Consequently, it has been, and is, used to improve the warmblood horse all over the world.

When the displays are over the serious buyers, and the inquisitive spectators, swarm through the stables to take another look at the young stock. They can ask to see them run up outdoors, on the edge of the racecourse. There the handsome 2½-year-olds trot around, showing off to everyone that they have exceptional temperament and that their trot is so extravagant, they need barely touch the ground.

The method of purchase is both curious and unique. Hopeful buyers can register a claim for any horse they like. Then, they draw, by ballot, a time for their meeting with the Hanoverian Society's commission. At these meetings they can discuss and bargain, but it is the commission not the purchaser, that is in control. The Hanoverian Society can direct who shall buy and, therefore, where the breed's stallions should stand. This does mean that they sacrifice higher prices, as auctions are a much more lucrative means of sale as was proven in 1975. The top price for a Trakehner that year was about £25,000, compared with the Hanoverian's £20,000.

It seems the private breeders of Hanoverians are a rare collection of people. They are willing to forgo income in the general interests of the breed. Not only is this system of sale accepted, but also the Hanoverian Society select the ten best horses for the state stud at Celle, and only pay the owners an average of £4,750 (1975). This is far below the market value for these, the best horses at the Hengstkörung. The owners accept this, partly because of the prestige of having their horses chosen to go to Celle, and partly because they know that it should help to raise the standard of the breed.

This curious process of sale is followed by an examination by a state (not breed) commission to decide which of the young stallions should be issued with licences. Those that are not successful have to be gelded. Consequently it is possible to have bought a gelding at this stallion market! In 1972, 76 Hanoverian 2½-year-olds were presented at the Hengstkörung and 60 were passed; but only 18 of the 61 Holsteins presented were passed, and 34 of the 85 Trakehners.

For those passed the next stage is performance tests, and only after these can a full licence be granted. It is not surprising, that with such a rigorous selection process the Germans are able to produce horses with the qualities they want.

The auctions

The purchasing system for riding horses is equally efficient. Most breeds run one to three auctions in a year. They are often great social occasions. The major sale for the Westfalian breed is held in October, at Munster, and has the atmosphere of a fair. The country comes to town as the sellers are mainly farmers who have spent weeks, months or even years preparing their prized equine specimens for this great occasion.

For the purchasers these auctions are a less risky way of buying than in Britain. In Germany they have the chance to carry out extensive tests on the horse before bidding. Veterinary examinations are possible, but most helpful of all, the horses can be ridden. At Munster there are two indoor arenas, one with jumps and another for work on the flat. Gleaming horses, with ornately braided manes, have rider after rider sit on them. The owners appear to be almost as good salesmen as are the Irish, giving high praise to the riders and extolling the virtues of their horse.

These trial sessions take place on the day before the bidding starts. On the day of the auction the horses are led into an enormous hall which is packed with spectators, many of whom are only there for the entertainment. They are not disappointed. The horses are usually ridden around the arena and in an effort to push the bidding up many a rider will show off his mount's dressage skills.

With the fair opportunity for purchasers to view the horses, prices can be very high. For a competition horse, £10,000 is not unusual and the average is over £3,000 (1975) for fashionable breeds.

The Hanoverian Society hold their auction at Verden. Like their Hengstkörung it is probably the most international of the auctions. They hold three, or more, auctions during the year but it is the October one that attracts the best horses and highest bidders. The horses in the catalogue give demonstrations in dressage and show jumping prior to the auction. These appear to dazzle buyers into paying high prices and, in 1975, about £20,000 was paid for an unproven 4-year-old.

Most of the horses purchased at these auctions stay in Germany, for the demand in this affluent country is high. But there are major foreign buyers. Italians do not limit their extravagant purchases to Ireland and in recent years their average annual import is about 1,000 horses from the Germans. The Belgians, too, have been big buyers in their efforts to establish themselves as a first-class equestrian nation. The Swiss, Dutch and Austrians are regular purchasers.

Unlike the French, the Germans are not greatly concerned about exporting horses. Their spirit of nationalism puts winning first. If importation is advisable to achieve this end, then it is, and has been, done. However, they do make it difficult to bring in second-rate competition horses by stipulating that imported jumpers and dressage horses must go straight into the middle of the top-grade events. Polish, Austrian, American, Swedish and Danish breeding horses are imported. But, it is from Britain that the most important blood is being bought. The Germans have become increasingly aware of the weakness of their breeds in eventing, as stamina has not been an aim for breeders. The Germans are not a nation to accept deficiencies, and they are now planning to correct those they find in their own breeds. The British have been most successful in eventing and so it is their thoroughbreds that the Germans want. In 1972, for example, 94 mares and stallions were bought from Britain.

The German horses are being fined down to suit modern needs. The old fashioned hefty type is being replaced. There is no doubt that with this broad minded, logical and rigorous approach to breeding that the Germans will add stamina to their horses' already proven assets of power, temperament, and movement.

RIDING CLUBS AND CENTRES

In all European countries the club plays a major role in a rider's life. In Germany it appears to be most important of all. Every rider has to be a member of a club and although the equestrian stars may outgrow them, they all started their riding through these organisations.

The German temperament rarely gains satisfaction from activities not involving improvement. They prefer to work at something, like dressage or jumping, in an indoor school or a permanent arena of a riding club. Apart from the odd farmer, few riders have horses in their own backyard, they keep them at

PLATE 5 (*above*)
The Riding School
at Verden. Such
luxurious facilities
are typical of those
found throughout
Germany.

PLATE 6 (*left*)
Reinstitut von
Neindorff.

PLATE 7

The DOKR centre at Warendorf, where leading dressage riders are warming up. In the foregound General Stecken talks to Karin Schlüter.

PLATE 8

Reiner Klimke and Hans Meyer in training at Warendorf.

their clubs. Nor does general leisure riding entail cross-country work.

This natural tendency has been reinforced by the law. Horseback riders are banned from going across country at will as they must restrict such jaunts to a scheduled number of paths. This has limited outdoor riding activities. One may feel sorry for the Germans. They miss the fun of traversing natural country, but this factor is balanced by the resulting development of the clubs into organisations of a very high standard.

Facilities rare in Britain are universal in Germany. Indoor schools, outdoor dressage and jumping arenas and cross-country fences are basic to nearly all clubs. Without the opportunity to learn riding the natural way, the German has to be taught. The benefit of this is that they learn to sit correctly, which makes controlling their horse easier and consequently large numbers of pupils find themselves enjoying dressage. Most clubs provide school horses, trained in lateral work and flying changes. Everyday riders have the opportunity, almost totally lacking in England, to experience on a trained horse what it feels like to execute relatively advanced movements. This experience is essential to a dressage education. So too is a good instructor and in Germany they are in abundance for there is a well developed, carefully planned and rigorous system for the production of trainers.

The Deutsche Reitschule

It is the Deutsche Reitschule which is the headquarters for the education of young trainers. It is on the outskirts of the German market town of Warendorf which is a few miles south-east of Munster. The school is approached down a narrow town street and the entire set-up is surrounded by houses. There is no room for cross-country fences, or outdoor jumping, but the Germans are keener on the hard concentrated work, which is best done indoors.

The indoor facilities of the Deutsche Reitschule would be difficult to improve on. There is a vast school, into which would fit two normal English schools, and this is usually divided so that two lessons can take place at the same time. There are a series of mirrors, long, high and clear enough for the rider to use them as a 'dumb trainer'. Additional conveniences include a water sprinkling system, a long gallery and a judges rostrum behind which are lecture rooms and offices.

Outside there is a small sand arena, where the riders occasionally take some fresh air, and an enormous barn full of stables. As elsewhere on the Continent the majority are stalls but the horses appear to be quite content to be tied with their faces to the wall. A few privileged ones are free in loose boxes. These are the top schoolmasters, but practically every horse in the barn is capable of lateral work and flying changes. Trained in the first place by the best students and instructors, they then become capable of educating the less able students. The danger of the schoolmasters' work deteriorating, with muddled inexperienced riding, is minimised by occasional brush up sessions with an instructor on board, and the hawk like eye of the trainer watching his students ride.

The DOKR

Less than a mile into the countryside from the Deutsche Reitschule is the most important establishment in German competitive riding, the centre run by the DOKR (German Olympic Committee). It seems the Kaiser was highly dissatisfied with the failure of German riders to win any gold medals at the 1912 Olympics. He created this committee in 1913 with the purpose of training riders to win medals. The First World War prevented the DOKR from having an immediate effect, but there has been no doubt about its success from the 1920s until the present day.

In the inter-war period the Germans took the Olympic team dressage gold medals in 1928 and 1932. In the Berlin Olympics they made a clean sweep, winning all the team and individual golds in dressage, jumping and eventing.

The Second World War, and its aftermath, entailed major re-adjustments for German riding. The cavalry school at Hanover, the backbone of German international success, was destroyed. The DOKR thought it sensible to take over the school's role. They built on the outskirts of Warendorf magnificent facilities in which their chosen riders could train, and bought them high class horses to compete on. Today, however, the stables contain only a few DOKR owned horses. The combination of high prices for top-class material and the desire of many top riders to have their own independent set-ups, led to the abandonment by the DOKR of an essentially cavalry type of approach. Civilian riders are different. Top-class individual riders just wanted facilities and trainers whose roles as diplomats and organisers are as important as their instructional ability.

For the young though, the training is still important and the DOKR has been flexible enough to allow for these different needs. Riders can stable permanently at the DOKR's centre. Martin Plewa, who was sixth in the 1973 European championship three-day event is there, as is Ewe Schullen Baunmler, a leading junior dressage rider, and probably the most famous of all German riders, Hans Günter Winkler. He has his own block of stables full of expensive and successful horses, and his own tack room where the walls are crammed with rosettes and plaques gained in his worldwide victories. Most of the other stables at the DOKR's centre are reserved for visitors who come for individual use of facilities or on one of the courses.

Visitors have outdoor facilities too. The cross-country riders have an ingeniously designed area of about one acre containing practically every type of cross-country obstacle. All these obstacles can be jumped from various directions and from each point of approach the problem varies both in severity and type. A rider can jump many, many times without asking the horse to tackle the same problem twice.

The show jumpers, too, have an outdoor arena, and there is a sand ring for all to use together with an indoor lungeing arena. Many of the top riders, especially the veterans of international competitions, come to use the facilities.

THE TRAINERS

Many of the top trainers in Germany have no qualifications, but most of the young people intent on making riding a career, go through the official system.

There are four levels of qualification. The groom, the professional rider, the riding instructor and the horsemaster. The first stage is to gain three years' experience in an authorised riding school. This is followed by a six-week course and an examination. Successful candidates become professional riders. This is followed

by another five years in a school, during which time they must
train a jumper and a dressage horse to medium level. They then
return on a three-month course and have to pass another examination before qualifying as an instructor. The highest qualification,
a horsemaster, requires more examinations and proven success
in training horses to high competitive standards. This emphasis
on competition is a feature of the German system, even the
professionals having to prove themselves in this sphere.

As yet, the official system has not produced any of the country's
national trainers. These are appointed by the DOKR in each of
the three Olympic disciplines. They have the dual function of
giving instruction, mainly for the benefit of the less knowledgeable young potentials, and of being *chef d'equipe* to the more
independent and experienced riders.

Herr Brinckmann

Hans Heinrich Brinckmann has filled the role of national
trainer in German show jumping since 1969. It is a difficult position for some question the value of training in this discipline.
In Germany although there are hundreds of dressage trainers,
there are only a few for show jumping. In common with most
countries, except America, it seems that the majority of star riders
get their help by exchanging advice between themselves. Hans
Winkler assists riders at the DOKR centre, Alwin Schockemöhle
has helped others, but it is more like applying a little polish than
serious training. It is a sport where perhaps character, grit and
natural talent are most important. Those who are thinking about
how to do things the correct way tend to suppress the more
important characteristic – the determination to clear the fence at
all costs.

Any national trainer in show jumping (with the exception of
Bertalan De Nemethy in America), has to come to terms with
this. The top riders develop their own ways and are reluctant to
be made to conform to a trainer's methods. Germany has been
clever in choosing Brinckmann as their national jumping trainer
and *chef d'equipe*. He understands the unwillingness of the stars to
be subjected to heavy training. He accepts this especially as he
knows he has a further indirect and powerful influence over the
way people ride because Brinckmann is the most famous course

builder in the world. He built the course for the 1972 Munich Olympics and the whole world looks to his every move, to learn from and adopt his techniques and methods.

Hans Heinrich Brinckmann is a friendly man with a shock of long white hair and is always moving quickly because he has much to do and wants to get on with it. He thinks he is a lucky man for he is deeply involved and enthusiastic about his job. He joined the cavalry before the war. In traditional cavalry fashion he tried his hand at everything – steeplechasing, eventing and jumping. But his orientation was towards show jumping, and he won Grand Prix competitions in Rome, Aachen, Amsterdam and Berlin in the years immediately before the Second World War.

Brinckmann has interesting reasons for choosing show jumping. He liked the challenge of training a jumper. To him, this meant establishing the closest possible relationship with the horse which needed both physical and psychological analysis. The horse's physical problems had to be studied, to find exercises and methods of overcoming them, and the horse's mind understood, so that horse and rider could become a single unit. He wanted to give his thinking to the horse.

A competition was another form of challenge. In little more than $1\frac{1}{2}$ minutes in the ring many problems have to be tackled and overcome. These are of an infinite variety. Each course is different, as is each arena, and for riders who jump in different countries, the adjustments needed are even more demanding.

For Brinckmann the prerequisite of establishing a partnership with a horse for jumping, was dressage. It was modified dressage, with the aim of creating a gymnast over fences. The exercises concentrated on were those which would overcome the weaknesses the horse showed when jumping fences. There was an exercise available from dressage for each problem, dressage simply being one lesson leading to the next, with the purpose of strengthening and developing each set of muscles until the horse was completely gymnastic.

For Brinckmann, dressage not only improved the horse's jumping ability, but it also prolonged the horse's life. If the rider relies only on the horse's power to get over the fence, without preparing and developing it, then the strains on the horse are enormous. He was sad that the pull of high prize money made riders bring their horses into the ring too quickly. Too often these horses were finished by the time they were 7 or 8 years of age. If only more preparation and training was done, they would be at their best during the prime age for a show jumper which is between 10 and 15 years.

Although Brinckmann varied the exercises for each horse, he thought every show jumper should be able to pirouette at the canter, complete flying changes and be able to show collection and extension of stride at all paces. He repeatedly emphasised that the object is to turn the horse into a better gymnast.

It was not just the horse, however, that had to be a gymnast. Brinckmann's particular contribution to training is a series of exercises for both the horse and the rider. He is conscious of the need of horse and rider to master their bodies. The first lesson is to involve his pupils in establishing a good riding position, and this is only possible if they have full control of their bodies.

From this basis he tries to develop in his pupils a 'sense' for the horse, the ability to give consistent aids combined with a thorough knowledge of dressage. It is this sense for a horse – horsemanship – which he feels is deteriorating. Excessive specialisation has meant that the all round horsemanship of cavalry officers is rare. For today's riders strength can become more important than sensitivity. He would like to see more show jumpers going across country or steeplechasing, so that they could get a feel for the natural ability of the horse to jump without domination.

Although enthusiastic about training, he recognised that his greatest influence had been in the sphere of course building. He has been able to design courses to get riders to jump his way. Consequently, when constructing his courses he tests more than jumping ability: the horse's handiness, balance and obedience, are on trial, as well as the ability of the rider to control his horse. In other words his (highly favoured) idea of whether horse and rider are masters of their bodies. In testing so many qualities he uses a great variety of problems and unlike most course designers uses both rather than either height or difficult distances as challenges for competitors. These problems though are never traps for his central aim is to get horse and rider going more confidently.

General Stecken

General Albert Stecken has been the corresponding national trainer in the dressage field, but now leaves most of the instructing to Herr Willy Schultheiss. The General concentrates on administration and acting as *chef d'equipe* to teams. He has a distinguished background for the position – a high rank in the German Air Force, and a family renowned for its horsemanship.

Stecken was brought up in one of the most famous German riding establishments – The Westfalian School in Munster. His father was chief instructor there and his brother Paul now holds the same position. The General, however, was to make his name in the field of judging. His great assets are perception and diplomacy, both of which have helped him to fulfil his difficult role as national dressage trainer.

Stecken is an affable, plump gentleman who seems to notice everything but deals with matters in a cool, calm, almost humble manner and frequently supports suggestions with jokes and smiles. This is clever tactics for temperamental stars are more easily dealt with when laughing than when serious.

Few would envy his position as *chef d'equipe* of the dressage prima donnas. He is usually dealing with very rich people, who have their own individual trainers and ways of doing things. Stecken accepts this and on a morning training session with twelve of the best German dressage riders he sat quietly in his rostrum passing comments over the loudspeaker. He developed more of a discussion than a one way authority. It was a fascinating form of training for at this stage the riders knew how to correct faults, what was needed was someone to point out when anything was going wrong – this was Stecken's great ability.

This role of mediator and adviser to these talented and widely differing riders now absorbs much of his energy, but he has other ambitions for the future. Since the end of the war and the destruction of the cavalry, training has been left in the hands of the individual. Different methods have emerged which he is unhappy about. In common with so many people, in so many countries, he wants to see his own style become more uniform. Stecken obviously dislikes excessive domination and use of strength. He wants to establish lightness and harmony as the stars to follow. These are uncommon aims in Germany where sturdy horses and determined riders tend to produce mechanical dressage. Stecken wants his riders to conform to the classical school – but he did add that in riding as everything else there is a difference between practice and the ideal!

The main points he mentioned in training were: for the rider, a light hand and a steady leg; for the horse, the establishment of suppleness, three good paces and balance. The balance, he liked his riders to work for with a long rein and to establish their horse's head in a deep position. This, together with his general approach, was more typical of the French than the German school. It seems most people support the ideals of the French approach, but the urge to win makes them sacrifice its full realisation. The more mechanical methods yield quicker results and are therefore tempting to adopt.

General Stecken's methods of achieving his aims are thorough. It is the young he is looking for. He wants to gather the inexperienced but talented at Warendorf and turn it into a civilian version of the Hanover cavalry school. He chooses riders with five or ten years' experience, who have shown promise in any aspect of riding, but have a special interest in dressage. He is setting up a talent spotting system at club, regional and national level. With this in operation Stecken hopes for both a more uniform style and the opportunity for the less well off riders to succeed.

With the established stars he wanted to create a more uniform approach bringing them together to have free discussions. He has met with remarkable success. He is responsible for twelve of the best riders performing a quadrille. This was a clever move. Not only does it entail the merging of individual idiosyncrasies to obtain a harmonious overall effect, but it has also shown to an increasing number of people the scope of German dressage talent. The Germans who saw this display performed at major events in Europe in the years immediately following the 1972 Olympics, must have been stirred to patriotic excitement that their riders could produce such an elegant and decorative demonstration. To the foreigner it is startling to see twelve riders from the same country performing good piaff and passage, and to know that there is a long reserve list of riders who could do almost as well. It proved Germany was head and shoulders above everyone else as a dressage nation.

Herr Schultheiss

In 1974 Willy Schultheiss was appointed the official DOKR trainer, to take up permanent residence at Warendorf. He is one of the cavalry schoolmaster, Otto Lörke's, most famous pupils, and after receiving this education he taught for many years the very successful German dressage rider Frau Springer. Now Schultheiss is following General Stecken's ideas and directing most of his talented instructional powers on the juniors of Germany. Courses are arranged regularly at Warendorf for the most able youngsters. It is interesting that Schultheiss has changed his tactics of training with these young stars. He used to instruct through riding the horse himself and only expecting his pupils to maintain rather than obtain the correct manner of going. Now he tells his young pupils how to achieve what is required, from the ground and rarely does it for them. Such an approach may take longer, but is likely to yield better horsemen for the future. Schultheiss' approach to training riders does not stop him from riding. He still brings on horses to sell or for his pupils. He is a maestro at producing horses in record time and at the 1975 Aachen show there were 7- and 8-year-old horses performing in the top classes that he had trained and sold.

Herr Theoderescu

Co-director, with General Stecken, of the quadrille and sympathetic to the General's ideas for lightening the German style, is George Theoderescu. It is not surprising, for this small man with an elfin face and a shock of fuzzy black hair, is not a German. He comes from Rumania, the communist country renowned for its attachment to France. Rumania's capital, Bucharest, is known as 'Little Paris' and Rumanian riders naturally follow the French school. The country has a long tradition of brilliant horsemen. They won the silver jumping medal at the Berlin Olympic Games in 1936. In the 1950s they ventured out again to compete against capitalist nations and in 1959 George Theoderescu was chosen for the team going to Aachen. However, when the rest of the team went home, he was not amongst them. This energetic, nonconformist gentleman could not face the restrictions of the Rumanian system. He bravely chose West Germany and freedom. Now his most severe restriction is not competing at any show near the border, or in Berlin.

When Theoderescu defected he was taken to Warendorf to work at the German Olympic committee's centre. It was there he met the girl who is now his wife. A handsome and friendly woman, Inge Theoderescu is the daughter of one of Germany's best course builders and a major stud organiser. She had had a comprehensive equestrian apprenticeship. She started as a trainer of young horses for the German, and then the English, army. She also learnt much about the ways of the ace show jumper Hans Winkler, her first husband. Then along came this refugee, a dressage rider who startled the Germans by taking off into the woods and jumping fences to get his horses' backs working correctly. She was won over by these ungermanic methods, and the Theoderescus now form one of the most successful partnerships in the dressage world. It is a working partnership. He rides her horse, she tells him if his horse's piaff is correct and there is a continual interchange of advice, assistance and encouragement.

Their first major venture was to pack their bags and head for the United States, but there they missed the German will to work and found it difficult to come to terms with many of the Americans. Like Gunnar Andersen the great Danish trainer, who succeeded them at the same American establishment of Jessica Newberry, they found riders who viewed their horse as a type of machine. Some Americans wanted to be told which button to push expecting everything to work like clockwork.

After two years the Theoderescus returned to Germany and rented an establishment south-west of Hanover. It consisted of an enormous barn-like indoor school with stables on either side and a heated sitting room where spectators could keep warm and watch the activities through a sliding glass window. The action is abundant. Riding starts at 6.30 a.m. and by this time the stables have been busy for one and a half hours. Theoderescu begins on his own having 6 or 7 horses to school before lunch. His wife arrives a little later – after the housework – and comes supplied with rolls and coffee for their breakfast. She had a mere 5 horses to train that morning. There are, however, 22 horses in their stables. Some are owned by them, but the majority belong to others and they are all there to be trained by, or under the guidance of, the Theoderescus. A professional rider working for his final examination exercises another half a dozen. Some young ones are lunged, others are ridden by the odd student.

Theoderescu confesses to preferring horse to human students, but his instruction is far too popular to enable him to concentrate on riding alone. Domini Lawrence and Penny Goring are two British riders who have spent time with him. The German junior team has been made his special province. The French clamour for the courses that he occasionally gives at the L'Etrier in Paris. The Dutch are just as keen to persuade him to come to their country as often as is possible.

This popularity rests on a number of assets. Firstly there is his broad base of knowledge. He was brought up by cavalry officers with French methods, which he has now combined with his experience of the German approach. This has resulted in a softer, lighter and more adjustable version of the highly successful German style. Secondly, he has an unusual ability to sit on a horse and immediately press those buttons the Americans found so elusive. His seat is exceptionally supple and deep, which produces great collection and a clear understanding with the horse. After a session with Theoderescu in the saddle students find they can ride their horses more easily. Finally as his wife said, 'We have fun when we work, we like riding horses'. He conveys this enthusiasm, enjoyment and informal approach to his pupils.

Visitors to his school quite often experience some calculated chaos. Dogs tear around the arena barking. Riders, on finishing their work, often turn their horses free which then career around. In the middle of all this the Theoderescus' tiny young daughter, whose legs are so short she can barely touch the horse, may be doing some single time changes. Theoderescu may be doing some piaff and stopping occasionally to give a few words of advice to a student. The seriousness and dourness of some German schools is not found here.

Another feature of the work at the Theoderescus' is that much of the riding is done without stirrups. Frau Theoderescu says she actually prefers riding without stirrups. Herr Theoderescu thinks he can get better piaff and passage without their support. That deep seat is not just an accident. Work without stirrups not only deepens the seat but strengthens the legs, and it is the legs rather than the hands that the Theoderescus rely upon. Too high a head position for instance is corrected with the legs, not the hands. They like the feel on the mouth always to be very light.

Theoderescu prefers to buy his horses unbroken and his wife claims he has the gift of looking at the frame of the horse, noticing which muscles should be developed and giving it the appropriate work to achieve this. Work starts on the lunge. Side reins are attached to the bit and many months are spent lungeing with the aim of getting the horse balanced at the three paces. Theoderescu values lunge work highly as it is a means of strengthening the neck, back and hindquarter muscles. This is also assisted by walking and trotting over poles on the ground so that the horse lowers his head and uses his hind legs. Then it is the turn of the rider to teach the horse to go forward, but always taking care not to make the horse bored. For the Germans this is more difficult. Horses in Germany are rarely turned out for a rest or freshening up periods. Three-year-olds come in and remain in work for most of their lives. The Theoderescus want the horses to enjoy their work as much as they themselves do. Variety is important so they take them outside, they go jumping and they work the horses with low and deep head carriage. This approach is hardly typical of the German school.

When the Theoderescus start the more serious work, the German approach becomes more apparent. They fully recognise the over-riding aim is to transfer the horse's weight on to its hind legs, making possible freer movement in front. This aim is in their minds at an early stage in the training and at all times ask the horse to place his hind legs well under him and so build up the muscles on the quarters. Even with young horses they ask for many halts to further collection. As soon as possible they start to work at the collected trot, accentuating the rhythm and slowly developing the passage. They frequently use the country-side to teach the most advanced movement – piaff. They have nearby a very steep sandy hill, which they take their horses down in order to get them to put their hind legs far underneath them.

In England some may say that they demand too much of the horse, at too early a stage, but Frau Theoderescu suggested that this point of view has contributed towards Britain's disappointing dressage performance. She felt that the English were too slow, they spent too much time in straightforward movements. Consequently they had difficulties in obtaining, for example, true collection. They tended to just shorten the stride, but not to obtain any elevation. Many of the horses were not suppple enough. These comments were much the same as the views of the Swede, Colonel Nyblaeus.

Herr Festerling

A trainer with a distinctively Germanic approach was Herr Festerling. He was in a position to perpetuate his ideas when, in the 1970s, he held the position of national trainer of instructors in Germany.

This role provided him with exceptional opportunities, for Germany is renowned for the high calibre of students entering the profession and for the intensive and long training they receive. It has made the atmosphere and approach at the Deutsche Reitschule, their training centre, similar to that of a university and Herr Festerling was their much revered 'Professor'. Ardent students followed this rotund gentleman wherever he moved, asking questions, carrying on discussions, and listening to every gem he might utter.

In general lessons there was little need for attentive listening. Herr Festerling ensured that everything was heard by bellowing his commands and harsh criticism. Quite often reinforcing this deafening noise by cupping his hands to his mouth. Then suddenly he would stop these terrifying outbursts and turn to talk quietly to his entourage of foot students. It was an interesting combination, this use of fear to get a message home, coupled with recurrent intelligent discussion.

Herr Festerling was a man with a purpose. He knew that his ideas and methods were the major influence on young German trainers. Consequently, he devoted much attention to them. But foreigners also come to Warendorf. It attracts young riders who want to learn and understand the ways of the most successful riding nation. Girls and boys come from Canada, Japan, Holland, England and America, pay their fees and, after helping in the stables, have about two rides a day on trained horses. Instruction they must grasp when they can. Potential instructors sometimes practise on them, and occasionally when Festerling was the chief he would stop concentrating on his own student instructors, to bellow some advice at these foreign visitors. But naturally he wanted to concentrate his energy on the students who were going to help his country. Foreigners who come to Warendorf learn by watching, and riding well-trained horses, but rarely from direct instruction.

Herr von Neindorff

A school offering greater opportunities and a warmer welcome to foreigners is Reinstitut von Neindorff. It is situated in the south on the edge of the sprawling industrial town of Karlsruhe. On the corner of one of the city's narrowest and most windy streets stands a large ornate old cavalry school. It looks out of place amongst its surroundings which are closely packed dingy houses and offices. The old cavalry school has been engulfed by suburban sprawl. Its proprietor too is out of place. Herr von Neindorff practises and approaches dressage in a way which few of his compatriots understand. He has none of that ruthless dedication and determination to win rosettes, money and glory with his dressage horses. Competitions to him are anathema as horses are ruined in the rush to perform difficult movements. His aim is to follow classical methods, to achieve harmony between horse and rider. He wants to make his horses more beautiful and his riders capable of expressing themselves through their horse.

Von Neindorff, lacking this competitive urge, is considered an eccentric in his country where winning is a near universal instinct. He is proud of, and helps to perpetuate, these differences between himself and so many of his fellow riders. To start with his appearance is strikingly individual. His coal-black hair is greased back to never come out of place. His enormous bulbous eyes watch everything. He looks like a film star of the twenties. His clothes, too, remind one of earlier times, for he always wears a short green jacket with dark green velvet lapels. Two alsatian dogs follow him everywhere and sit in the corner of the school when he is riding, but, like their owner, they do not bite or bark. This rather imposing effect cloaks a calm, thoughtful personality. His many pupils respect him, not out of fear, for he never raises his voice, but for the clear way he has thought out his ideas, for his adherence to these, for his great ability as a rider, and for the unique and unusual atmosphere he creates.

Von Neindorff was born into an equestrian minded family in

what is now East Germany. His father was a General in the cavalry, and the young von Neindorff was able to learn from the authorities of the time. However, it was Zeimer, from the Spanish Riding School, who was the greatest influence on him and it is the classical principles which he promotes at his Reinstitut.

During earlier years his disdain for competitions had not developed. After the Second World War he became one of Germany's leading dressage riders, and was a runner up in the German championships. Age brought disillusionment with this form of dressage and, in 1954, he decided to retire from competitive activities in order to concentrate on pure teaching.

Von Neindorff teaches dressage as an art, not a craft, and the surroundings at the Reinstitut help to accentuate this approach. The indoor school was built with an eye for decorative effect as well as practicability and there are pretty high arched windows. Towards one end there are pillars donning orange and red flags, surrounded by potted flowers.

There is no gallery and von Neindorff normally sits in a small glass-fronted cubicle. From here he controls his class and plays classical music to suit the mood he wants to create. He speaks in beautiful German through a microphone and sometimes becomes so involved that he acquires a sing-song tone. The lighting is also used to create effect. Sometimes the pillars are spotlighted and the rest of the school kept in darkness, sometimes all lights will blaze. The classical music, the decorative school and the prose that he uses to express his instructions turn it into a type of theatrical production. Riding becomes, as von Neindorff wants, a form of art.

Although von Neindorff is the producer and director it is the horse, rather than the rider, that is the actor. In the stables von Neindorff has over 40 horses of his own. He has collected them from all over the world. They include Andalusians, East Prussians, Swedish, Hanoverians, Lipizzaners, Czechoslovakians and English thoroughbreds. He has trained them himself, and most can perform piaff and passage after a few years' work. These horses are his means of teaching pupils. Von Neindorff can sit in his cubicle, looking out upon a class of up to 14, mounted on his handsome trained stallions. He can explain to his class the reasons for the mechanism of a movement and the aids to apply. Then, on the word of command which the horses seem to recognise, the whole class goes into half pass, half pirouettes or some other movement. Naturally the figure has been pre-planned, so the effect is like a musical ride. There are few individual corrections from him, for he believes that a rider on a trained horse can learn to sit well and give the right aids.

The pupils who subject themselves to this rather eccentric but fascinating training vary enormously. When I was there a 91-year-old doctor regularly rode one of the stallions. There were, too, housewives who came for an hour or two and dedicated riders who have become Neindorff converts. They had abandoned competition work to spend as much time as possible in his school. In addition there is a continuous influx of students, from all over the world, but mainly from America, Canada and Britain. Then there is the occasional competition rider wanting to discover the art, rather than the technique, of dressage. The Canadian dressage rider, Mrs. Christine Boylen, spent many months there before the 1972 Olympic Games.

Outside the old cavalry school is a smaller indoor arena, where the young horses are trained and the riding for beginners takes place. In another corner, crammed in on two sides by houses, are the stables. Some are brick barns with lines of stalls and loose boxes, but there are also rough wooden and tin stables hurriedly constructed to meet an influx of horses. Von Neindorff is a collector of beautiful horses. He cannot resist buying with the aim of turning them into even more elegant creatures through his work. Including those belonging to his pupils, there are some 80 horses housed in this hotchpot of stables. Other creatures wander through including goats and children. The atmosphere is informal, but the work hard. Working pupils, mainly from Germany and America, look after between 8 and 11 horses each, and often only get their ride after 7 p.m. But they are happy. They are amongst like-minded people, wanting to acquire as much knowledge as possible from their revered master von Neindorff, and his horses.

The piece of knowledge that he is for ever re-stating is that it takes time. Training horse and rider involves going through a logical series of stages and those who miss any steps will pay the penalty later. The most important point for von Neindorff is to build upon a solid basis. For the rider this means a deep seat. Only

PLATE 9
Josef Neckerman, riding one of his Olympic horses, Antoinette.

PLATE 10
The Germans acquire their deep seats by hard work. Reiner Klimke the world champion riding in.

PLATE 11
Alwin Schockemöhle, the 1976 Olympic champion, probably the most famous protagonist for the use of the draw rein demonstrates its use.

then is it possible to give clear, co-ordinated aids which enable the horse to understand what is required of him. The rider acquires this on a well-balanced horse, on the lunge with an instructor asking for: firstly, a straight line through the back of the shoulder, elbow and heel; secondly, quiet hands which can maintain delicate contact and at all times remembering hands are only an extra—it is the legs that control; thirdly, legs when not in use should lie so quietly that they can feel the breathing of the horse. The knee and the heel must be as low as possible and the seat bones always in contact with the saddle. The rider must sit in, not on, the horse. Finally, there is the need for suppleness in the shoulders, elbows and arms, so that they can follow the movement of the horse. The hips must be able to swing delicately, but suppleness is most important of all in the small of the back. It must be possible to tense the muscles in this area independently to give aids to the horse and to relax in order to absorb movement. Von Neindorff's riders have to be able to co-ordinate not just hands and legs but also the small of the back. By giving, taking and constantly adjusting these three, the rider can establish a steady and lasting connection with the horse.

It will, as he always points out, take time. It needs a develop-ment of muscles, good health, understanding, diligence, persis-tence, knowledge of the subject and, above all, kindness to the horse. It is pupils with these assets that von Neindorff is looking for, not ones seeking rapid results and immediate success.

Pupils with wonderful seats are one feature of Reinstitut von Neindorff, another is that few horses trained there cannot achieve piaff and passage. This is due, von Neindorff says, to building on a solid basis. It is worth noting that the one horse who could not achieve piaff or passage when I was there, was a thoroughbred. Young horses spend their first 1 to 1½ years on the lunge with side reins (in common with, but for a longer period than, other continentals). Then it is the turn of the rider whose aims are to develop correct basic paces, balance, active hind-quarters, impulsion and suppleness. When this has been done, it will be easy to master more complicated movements. Too much haste makes the horse inflexible, force becomes necessary and this is no longer classical dressage. The horse must only be asked to do what he is capable of. Von Neindorff also rejects tricky refinements. He is only interested in natural, not circus, movements. For example, changes every stride are frowned upon at the Institute as unnatural.

In keeping with von Neindorff's insistence on never asking for anything which is unnatural, or beyond the horse's capabilities, is the importance given to relaxation. Fresh horses are made to stand still, rather than work hard. All horses spend much time at the halt, the rider feeling them with hands and legs to obtain their concentration and to get them to relax their back. Many of the exercises (such as the half pass) are frequently done at the walk. As soon as horses are tired they are given a long rein. They are never made to work too hard or too long.

The result of this building on a solid basis and of not demanding too much, is that many of von Neindorff's horses are still working well at 20 years of age. It also means there is a tendency towards specialisation. Horses are used for the movements at which they shine. Hence pupils can sit on a Lipizzaner that will give them a good feel of piaff and levade, and on a Hanoverian to get a feel of the extended trot. With these experiences stored in their mind they know what to aim for when training other horses.

The work of the school, the ability of von Neindorff to produce both dedicated riders with good seats and gymnastic horses, is displayed to the public twice a year. Again he follows his principles, the 6 horses and their lady riders are not asked to perform an established reprise, as at the Spanish Riding School. Instead they only do what each horse is capable of on that day.

Bubi Gunther

The trainer who practised a more characteristically German style than either the Theoderescus or Herr von Neindorff, unhappily died in 1974. However, his influence will be felt for many years as he was responsible for training more successful riders than anyone else. Today's best young trainers, such as Herbert Rehbein, spent time under him. Also riders who queued up to obtain his services are still going to practise his methods. His name was Bubi Walter Gunther and he was often referred to, with a mixture of affection and timidity, as 'zee boss' or 'god'.

Bubi Gunther was the wrong shape for dressage. He was short and very round. His face was expressive and continuously changed shape and colour as he roared at a pupil, or broke the deathly atmosphere he had thus created with a wisecrack. But much of his teaching was done through riding. This extraordinarily rotund figure merged into the horse and he seemed able to obtain instant obedience.

Bubi Gunther's riding career began in show jumping. He won many international classes and his wife Maria was the lady champion of Germany. His training of jumpers, however, entailed advanced dressage work as they were taught piaff and pirouettes to make them supple and quick to turn. He felt this was a much better way of obtaining obedience than through the use of gadgets.

In the early 1960s he began to concentrate more on dressage. The number and stature of his pupils grew rapidly. He found himself travelling all over Germany to advise and help the top names in dressage. He was the only man to receive this universal approbation as it is the practice in Germany for each top rider to have their own personal trainer. Bubi Gunther was unique in having enough prestige to oversee each and every one of them.

He did not invent new ideas or approaches. He practised the German style with the horse strongly on the bit and highly flexed. His horses were given neither the length of rein nor the lightness of contact advocated by the French. A rider could only adopt this approach if they had a deep seat, when all the weight could be put in the saddle to help activate the horse's hind legs. He practised an extreme version of the German style where the emphasis is on forcing the hind legs to work, rather than aiming first and foremost, as the French do, at forward movement and impulsion.

Bubi Gunther's schooling was very hard. It involved much halting and going directly forward again. The horse's exercise, however, was over quickly and there were no confusions. His great gift was clarity so that the horse could understand quickly what was required of him. The rewards were there if the horse obeyed and the punishment too if he did not.

Humans also benefited from such clarity. The horses were taught to do a movement correctly with Bubi Gunther in the saddle. He would then expect good results from his pupils when they tried. Even the great dressage stars were subjected to tirades if they did it wrong, but to praise and fun if it was correct. It was obviously an effective way of training, but there are few that can practise it. Only a great horseman can make a horse understand so clearly what is right and wrong and again, so clearly, make a rider know what is required of him.

Bubi Gunther's young horses were brought on quickly as there was no confusion from muddled aids. He liked to teach them in the form of play; he said it should be like a children's kindergarten school. They were given an inclination of not what arithmetic, reading and writing were about but passage, half passes and shoulder in. He would ask for collection occasionally, so that at about 6 years they would learn the passage without effort. He would let them do lateral work, to prepare them and supple them up. But it all had to be fun, he only demanded their best effort later on. This was much the same approach that the Swede, Stig Claesson practised.

Hans Günter Winkler

Hans Günter Winkler is most famous as a rider. He has five Olympic gold medals to his credit, which is more than any other rider. He has competed in nearly one hundred Nations Cups—more than anyone else. He has won two World championships, and one European. He has won Britain's King George V Cup twice. Yet he shines too as a trainer and he helped many of Germany's leading riders, including Alwin Schockemöhle, Herman Schridde and Fritz Ligges.

This rather unathletic looking German, who has to wear glasses when riding, was born in 1926. He did not take up jumping until the end of the Second World War, when he was in his twenties. He was quick to realise the shortcomings of the, then, existing German style. They rode heavy horses over high fences, but were unable to challenge the speedy French and Spanish in timed jump offs. Hans Winkler visited the Italian Cavalry School at Pinerolo, which Caprilli had made world famous. This gave him an insight into a more sympathetic and forward going style. He evolved from this education, and by watching the riders of other nations, a method and style of jumping which he has been true to ever since.

His greatest horse was the half bred trotter mare, Halla. Together they won three Olympic gold medals, and two World championships. Since then he has had a string of successful horses – Fidelitas, Fortun, Enigk, Jagermeister, Torphy, who have won for him continental championships and gold medals.

Hans Winkler stables his horses at Warendorf, in the German Olympic Committee Training Centre. He uses these facilities for his own use and to help other riders. Winkler refers to this help not as teaching, but as advising, talking and giving his routine to other people. In this way, at Warendorf in the 50s and early 60s, he polished the stars of today, Alwin Schockemöhle and Fritz Ligges. The next generation, however, have made less use of his mind and experience. Shows now run from January to December, and Hans Winkler says the young have little time for training. Accordingly he has diverted more of his energies towards business, in which he is a public relations officer.

Hans Winkler has positive ideas on the training of riders and horses. With the riders he likes to aim for a standard style. He feels that, if left to develop individually, faults and bad habits arise too easily. But there must be a compromise, for he is aware of the dangers of suppressing individual brilliance in favour of a standard style and, after all, his two star pupils practise very different approaches to jumping. There is the classical sympathetic style of Fritz Ligges and the strong disciplinarian approach of Alwin Schockemöhle.

In the training of horses Hans Winkler starts from the premise that he is dealing with a German horse. The latter's greatest asset is not the class of the thoroughbred, nor the dash of the French Selle Français, but power. The most important thing is to control this power and then the horse can be made more machine like than any other horse. They can be made to do everything exactly as the rider requires it – from reaching their peak of readiness for the most important event (such as the Germans' consistent ability to win the Olympics) to arriving on exactly the right point for take off.

Control is Hans Winkler's operative word. It is a mathematical, analytical approach to jumping. All his horses learn a relatively high standard of dressage to achieve his principal aim of absolute obedience. Suppleness and good paces are secondary to this.

Again, when jumping, 'control' is the important word. Hans Winkler contains his horse until he can judge exactly the right place to take off. Then he accelerates with great force towards this point, giving his horse plenty of impulsion to jump the fence.

The interesting point is that this demand for control and obedience does not entail suppression of the horse's character. Hans Winkler's horses must still be able to think for themselves. At first this would appear contradictory, but Winkler riding Halla demonstrated his point dramatically at the 1956 Olympics. He completed the first round over the most formidable Olympic course ever built, with a mere 4 faults, but over the last fence he pulled a muscle. For the second round Winkler had to be carried to his horse because he was in such severe pain. In such a state he was incapable of doing much else than steering. But Halla had been thoroughly trained and she responded to his lightest aid, and she still knew how to think for herself. They were able to jump the bravest clear round in the history of show jumping. It brought them, too, gold medals as an individual and as members of the team. This was vindication of Hans Winkler's training methods.

ADMINISTRATION AND COMPETITION

The administration of all competitions in West Germany is the responsibility of the National Federation (FN). Their offices, like the Deutsche Reitschule and the Olympic Committee's Centre, are at Warendorf. It is a vast organisation covering breeding as well as competing, and the volume of work is such that they have their own computer.

In 1968 the Federation was rationalised into three divisions for sport, breeding and membership. All their activities are financed largely by the government and to some extent by the sale of publications and membership fees. This government finance means there is no need to rely on running shows to obtain income, as is the case in Britain.

The FN may not run shows but it does control them. All category A shows which are those offering a total of more than 300DM prize money, in one class, must be registered with them. The remaining small events are registered with special commissions in each state. At these, category A shows, the horses are divided into four grades L, LM, M and S (highest). Upgrading takes place when a horse has won five times in a category and prize money is not considered.

The interesting feature is that registration and grading are integrated for the three types of equestrian sports. There is no separation, or different systems. The 7,000 (1974) horses registered with the FN can all compete in dressage, eventing and jumping. They are upgraded from L to M after winning five events, dressage, or jumping competitions.

The other notable aspect of this registration system is that pedigrees have to be given. German warmbloods are treated in the same way as are thoroughbreds. Pedigrees have been kept for many generations and are given considerable weight when evaluating a horse.

Show jumping

Show jumping in Germany is big business and for competitors it is a demanding full-time activity. There is a constant succession of shows and the rest period has been reduced to a mere 6 weeks over Christmas. The successful are richly rewarded as the prize money, about three-quarters of which is sponsored, is high. There is additionally another major source of income and that comes from the sale of horses. The top riders know that there is a market for good horses and, in an affluent Germany, many people are eager and able to own expensive horses that will be ridden by high ranking international competitors.

Show jumping is second only to football in popularity. The activities and success of the riders is public news which gives great prestige and amusement to owners. They tend to be business men with little desire for close personal contact with their equine property. They buy horses for vast sums (up to £100,000 is said to have been paid) and leave them in the stable of the seller. Thus many of the top riders find themselves in the happy position of having both the money and the horse.

The most prolific owner of this type is Dr. Herbert Schnapka, an importer of Russian oil. He owns about 30 of the best horses in Germany. Although he has a stud with magnificent equestrian facilities amongst the rolling hills around his home at Nehmten, most of his show jumpers are in the top riders' stables scattered around Germany.

The 1974 World champion, Hartwig Steenken, rode Simona for him. Paul and Alwin Schockemöhle, Herman Schridde, Gerd

Wiltfang, Fritz Ligges and Lutz Merkel all have the odd priceless horse in their own stables belonging to Dr. Schnapka. Eddie Macken the Irish runner-up in the 1974 World championships was also a recruit. For the 1975 season he lured him away from Ireland so that he could ride his horses and work at Nehmten.

There are other rich owners trying to buy the best horse and have the best rider on board. Werner Stockmeyer, the sausage magnate, has horses with both Lutz Merkel and Sönke Sönkson. But it is not always a smooth path. Gerd Wiltfang chose as an owner a property tycoon, Herr Kun who went bankrupt for many millions. Wiltfang watched his horses go into a dispersal sale. Askan, his King George V Cup winner and his partner in the winning team at the Munich Olympics, was one who was to fall into other hands.

The existence of rich owners demanding only top jockeys, means Germany tends to be dominated by a dozen riders. They have stables housing a string of horses, but rarely owning more than the odd youngster which they are polishing up for sale. There is the odd exception. Hendrik Snoek rides his own horses. He is one of the few riders who was born rich, but he has adopted a carefully devised plan to make best use of this finance. He and his family have built up their own source of jumpers. They run a stud with stallions and mares of proven jumping blood. They produce 10 foals a year and find little need to buy established and expensive jumpers. They usually have 30 odd horses in work. Hendrik has the pick of these, Marian his sister, a European junior champion, rides another 3 or so. The remainder are brought on by the working pupils. The odd one is sold, but Hendrik and Marian have replacements readily available.

The other major difference between the Snoeks and their compatriot international riders, is that in between shows they are involved in serious outside work. Hendrik is an Economics graduate (it takes 5 years in Germany) and now works in his father's successful company. Schooling sessions take place after work and often the lights blaze in the indoor school until 8 p.m.

Another rider who breeds show jumpers is Paul Schockemöhle. However, this is a commercial operation and not a means of supplying himself with mounts. He sells much of the stock before it is broken and has in his yard many horses belonging to the rich owners of Germany. Abadir, Agent, Talisman, all belong to Dr. Schnapka.

Alwin Schockemöhle, the handsome elder brother of Paul, has been the second most important rider to Winkler, both success-wise and as an influence over the German methods of riding. Born in 1937 he came under Hans Winkler's tuition at Warendorf at the age of 17. He had the unusual record of being reserve to both the event and jumping teams at the 1956 Stockholm Olympics. By 1960, however, he had concentrated on jumping and was a member of the victorious team in Rome. From this time onwards he registered continuous successes with such horses as Ferdl, Donald Rex, Rex the Robber and Warwick. But it was not until 1975, after nearly two decades of being a mainstay of the German team, he eventually won an individual title. He became the 1975 European champion, in addition to winning the King George V Cup. Then in 1976 he won the ultimate honour, on Warwick at Montreal he became the Olympic individual gold medallist.

Apart from the horses and a farm, Alwin Schockemöhle has interests in 3 steel companies at Bremen, Vechta and Mulheim. This all round success is no surprise for he is one of the most thought-ful and clever of the international riders. He has followed Winkler's principles to a further extreme than their proposer. He is a dressage devotee and he makes great demands on his horses, endeavouring to make them extremely loose, supple, obedient and light in the hand. He has become famous for his schooling with the draw rein bringing the horse's head low on to its chest, and adopting a see-saw action with the reins to make the head move from side to side. The aim of this severe form of training is two-fold. Firstly, it loosens the horse's back and neck and secondly, it makes the horse use its hocks, thereby strengthening its hind-quarters and releasing the power for which the German horses are famous.

In the ring, too, Alwin Schockemöhle practises a more extreme version of Winkler's methods. He collects the horse much more between fences and accelerates harder into them, releasing his horse's head on the last 3 or 4 strides.

Alwin Schockemöhle has, in his turn, helped other young riders. His star pupil has been Gerd Wiltfang, whose first major success was the German championship in 1966. Wiltfang's greatest victories have been on Askan for whom a record price, at the time, of £56,000 was paid. Gerd Wiltfang has moderated Schockemöhle's approach to ride more evenly and sympathetically. He is renowned for having some of the best 'hands' in international jumping.

Germany's 1974 World show jumping champion – Hartwig Steenken – is another, who does not demand obedience in too obvious a manner. This rather shy and undemonstrative German who runs a stud farm at Mehlendorf, quietly and very determinedly, just gets on with the business of winning. With Simona he has to his credit a 1972 Olympic team gold medal and both the 1972 European and 1974 World championships. With Porta Westfalica, Kosmos and Erle he has won major international competitions.

Obedience, however, is the basis of German riding. Even Hendrik Snoek who prides himself on a more English approach to riding said that 'horses may be able to think for themselves, but I prefer to have them obeying what I think'. The other feature of German jumping is this obsession with activating the hindquarters. To achieve this, draw reins are in frequent use and rigorous training is essential. Fun and outdoor work are rarely a part of a German show jumper's programme. The indoor school and the jumping arena are usually the only place of exercise.

The German style and approach to jumping has evolved because it suits the temperament of the German rider and the type of competition horse they have bred. Riders are self disciplined, determined, strong and firm. This makes possible the exacting and demanding nature of the style they have adopted. The horses have great power and scope but they do not have the natural impulsion or lively nature of thoroughbreds. They need disciplined training to produce their ability and, because of their good temperaments, are able to accept it. The German horse and rider suit each other well.

The Germans are a supreme jumping nation. They have developed a style of riding and a breed of horse which has won for them Olympic team gold medals in 1956, 1960, 1964 and 1972. It is natural with this success in the ultimate test of show jumping that other nations have sought the secrets of their methods. They have studied their style, bought their horses and have copied their courses. Ideas of the national course designer, Brinckmann, are studied and re-enacted in many other countries. Naturally he builds fences that suit the Germans. The obstacles have become massive and formidable in appearance and more difficult to knock down. They have become wider and higher. Only a brave horse with great scope will attack them. At the same time the upright obstacle which needs a careful horse and precision riding to clear, has become rarer. As long as the emphasis in course building is on the size and formidability, rather than precision and careful jumping, the Germans must start favourites for the Olympic Games.

Dressage

Dressage in Germany is not an underdog sport that one might expect considering the popularity of jumping. Jumping competitors themselves know enough about it to understand and respect the dressage participants. The spectators have been educated to dressage through their own riding, television programmes, newspapers and books. They know what to look for in the tests and it has become, especially at the higher levels, a spectator sport. Sometimes the free style test is marked by the judges exposing their points on boards, as in ice skating, and they are frequently greeted with boos or cheers according to the views of the informed spectators.

Frequent competitions, high remuneration and the prestige value of dressage has attracted many participants. So many in fact, that the FN has had to shorten the tests to enable the shows to get through their programmes. It is not only at the lower levels that the entries are vast. A Prix St. George class may receive 50 entries and in the country as a whole there are about 250 people who can ride to that standard. Juniors (18 to 20) are swarming to take up dressage. In 1974 in a class restricted to horses owned and ridden by Westfalian residents and in which they were asked to do flying changes and half passes there were 60 to 70 entries.

As in show jumping the rich have been attracted towards this prestige sport. But there is a major difference; most of them are participants. At the top competitions in Germany the classes are dominated by professionals and the well to do, most of the latter riding horses prepared for them by their personal trainers. As in show jumping most of the successful competitors are those who practise mass production. The homes of the victorious dressage riders usually have indoor schools that make Stoneleigh look like a local barn. The stables are normally full of horses wiich keep the yard's private professional busy training all day, and provide a constant supply of top class material for their owner. It is a system which demands affluence and planning, but still takes German determination and discipline to be made such good use of.

Liselott Linsenhoff, the Munich individual Olympic gold medallist, has been at the top of the dressage world for a long time. Her first individual Olympic medal – a bronze – was won at Stockholm in 1956. She has that fortunate combination of assets – riding ability, meticulous determination and wealth. Britain's junior dressage riders invited to go on a course at her establishment in 1974 were amazed that any private individual could have such luxurious and prolific facilities. Everything was the 'best' that could be built. Herbert Kuchluch is her professional trainer and whilst he is not the most famous, he is one of the most knowledgeable. Like Thiedemann and Schultheiss he studied under the former cavalry master Otto Lörke.

Becoming the most sought after professional is the young Herbert Rehbein, who was trained by Bubi Gunther. His star pupil is Karin Schlüter and the horses they both ride are now owned by Herr Schulte Frohlinde who has built a lavish new dressage centre on the northern outskirts of Hamburg.

The pretty blonde Karin Schlüter has been on teams that have won silver Olympic team medals, European and World championships, but even with this experience she relies upon a trainer's help. Many of the horses, of this very slim lady, are very heavy. A strong capable man is needed to collect them. On one occasion Frau Schlüter was dissatisfied with the passage she was attempting. Rehbein was there to take over. He jumped on – his seat so deep it appeared glued to the saddle, his tummy stuck so far forward he looked a little like humpty dumpty. The horse immediately went perfectly for him. Those watching passed a few remarks about how good he was, and by the expression on his face, I do not think he would have disagreed.

The richest and most famous of the dressage riders and owners is Josef Neckerman. He has six Olympic medals to his credit (two gold) and two World championships. Neckerman's luxurious equestrian establishment is close to Frankfurt. He is a self-made millionaire who earned his fortune from a chain of shops of the Marks and Spencer variety. His first competitions were in the show jumping arena. He was unlucky, he had a few accidents and received an increasing number of suggestions from his bank manager to take up a safer activity.

Neckerman turned to dressage, and set about it in a typical businesslike fashion, with success as the target. He bought trained and proven potential Olympic horses, spent about a year adjusting them to his riding, then produced them in the arena with consistent success. He did buy young horses but he billeted them out with the best professionals until they approached international standard, then he would take them over.

Neckerman now restricts his competitive activities, but his daughter Frau Eva Maria Pracht is upholding the family dressage interest. In 1974 she won the John Pinches International Championship at Goodwood (U.K.). This petite and pretty lady is a picture on her horse, but again needs a strong capable professional to make the German horse obedient. Heinz Lammers does this for her, and also trains Edith Master the American Olympic rider.

Reiner Klimke is one of the few great dressage riders with no professional attached to his stable. This tall thin lawyer's earliest equestrian competitions were in the eventing field. Today he takes pride in a family approach and his wife competes and trains to Grand Prix level. Their results are impressive and the stable is full of top horses. Reiner Klimke does have, however, a source of help if necessary. He is the president of one of Germany's top riding schools, the Westfalian at Munster. The riding master there is Paul Stecken, brother of the General, Albert. Klimke has been able to make use of both the facilities of the school and the advice of Paul Stecken.

With Neckerman cutting down on his competitive activities, Klimke became Germany's dressage leader, captaining the team that won the 1976 Olympic gold medal. In 1974 he won the individual title in the World championships. Before this he helped Germany to win two team dressage gold medals at the Olympics and in 1973 was European champion. Now he is passing on his experience. Hans Jurgen Meyer, a winner of the German youth dressage championship, and probably the most talked about young rider in the 1974 World championships, spends much time at the Klimke establishment.

The handsome Harry Boldt has no professional helping him either, but his father was an instructor and provided a ground-work of knowledge. Although an amateur he usually rides horses for other people, practising a lighter, more sympathetic style than most of his compatriots. Apart from being a long-standing member of victorious German teams at both the Olympics and World championships, he has won major individual honours. In 1975 he was runner-up in the European championship and in 1976 became the individual silver medallist at the Montreal Olympics on Woycek, nor was this the first for in 1964 he had won the silver on Remus.

These German dressage riders naturally vary in their approach, but they have one feature in common. A deep and highly effective seat. They make much more use of this aid than the riders in other countries. Their backs are so straight they would shine in a deportment class. They use this posture to pass constant messages through their seat bones to make the horse activate his hindquarters.

The other feature of the German riding is the obedience they demand. They remove more of the 'will' of the horse than riders from other nations. The Germans are proud people; they know they can do it and very little will stop them from persuading the horse to do it. They demand much, difficult movements are part of everyday work, relaxing activities are rarely considered; and they can demand so much because their horses have sensible temperaments, and because they ride so competently, so precisely, that the horse understands what is required.

The horses are not the only ones that work hard. Those effective seats and ability to give clear aids come after hours spent without stirrups; most riders accompanying this practical work with a serious study of the technique of dressage. But for Germans, work is natural, for they know it is the best means of achieving success.

German dressage riders have won the gold or silver team medal at the last six Olympics, and have always collected a few individual medals. Although in 1976 the star of the Games – Christine Stuckelberger – came from Switzerland her style and methods are German and her horse came from Germany. There are many who would like to see riders with a freer style of dressage receive higher honours. But there are no great exponents of this today. The French are suffering a dressage depression. The Swedes, who practised modified free riding, are similarly going through lean times. The Russians are the only nation to offer a consistent challenge and their style is little freer than the Germans. The Germans are simply the best riders, whether or not one is sympathetic towards their degree of accuracy and precision.

Three-day eventing

Eventing is the one equestrian discipline in which the Germans are not the best. They do win medals and continental championships, but England and America must be considered their superiors. In the jumping and dressage phases they are as good as any, but it is in the cross-country that they make mistakes. Their riders find it difficult to master this form of riding, having spent so much of their life inside arenas. Nor to the horses excel, for German breeders, until recently, put little priority on stamina.

The Germans are not ones to display weaknesses for long. English horses, of the class of Chicago and Benson, have been imported at great cost to compete on. Also, for the long term, more thoroughbred blood has been injected into the breeding system. The German horses (especially the Hanoverian) is acquiring more class. In the 1973 European championships at Kiev, the Germans were mounted on home-bred horses. They won the team award and Herbert Blocker on Albrant took the individual silver medal. However they were unable to repeat this performance at the 1974 World championships or the Olympic Games where the Americans re-asserted their supremacy.

On the training side, too, there are deficiencies. Few Germans excel as instructors of eventers. Lars Sederhom, the English based trainer, has been brought over on occasional courses to Dr. Schnapka's equestrian centre at Nehmten. Karl Schultz their Olympic individual bronze medallist at Montreal came to England for a whole season in order to make use of the English system. However it is not entirely a one way traffic. English event riders pay visits to Germany. Richard Meade has been amongst those who have spent time with Germany's top trainer Ottokkar

Pohlmann at his school at Deining near Munich. Pohlmann was an international event rider himself, and now as a trainer he is recognised as the most successful in Germany.

The event riders of Germany have an additional problem. Unlike dressage and jumping the competitive opportunities are limited. There are three-day events but one- and two-day events are less frequent than in Britain. It is difficult to compete more than once a month without travelling great distances. Instead the event riders tend to gain their experience by competing regularly and successfully in the specialised disciplines, the jumping and dressage competitions. This is perhaps yet another reason why they are weak in the one sphere they can practise less easily, the cross-country.

Driving

As in Switzerland, driving in Germany has been a major competitive sport for some time. At their CCIO – Aachen, driving has been one of the feature events, and the first World driving championships were staged at Munster in 1972. In fact it has been a traditional part of German horsemanship. Most of the schools boast of both riding and driving opportunities, although few have extensive facilities for the latter.

The most comprehensive courses for driving are run by the regional governments. The Westfalische Reit-und Fahrschule at Munster, for example, organises a month-long course, starting throughout the year. Although driving is only part of the curriculum on these courses, it can be specialised in. Increasing numbers of foreigners attend, as Germany is one of the few countries offering opportunities to learn to drive.

Children

The children of Germany are brought up with a different approach towards riding than are those of the British. Hunting, gymkhanas, polo and other, natural, fun ways of learning are rare activities there. Instead, most of the time is spent in indoor and enclosed arenas. Until recently, training began mainly on horses, but there has been a great expansion in use of, and demand for, the pony. With this serious concentrated approach to riding the young acquire excellent seats and tackle problems with their brains rather than their instinct. Dressage and jumping, rather than galloping across country, become their dominant interests.

The children's prime competitive activity is vaulting. This pastime is rare in England, but it is an ancient practice. The Romans used gymnastics as part of their basic training of horsemen. In the 1920 Olympic Games it was part of the equestrian activities. Now it is a fast growing sport for the children of Europe, with international championships.

The horse is lunged at the canter. Side reins are attached to a vaulting surcingle. This has two handles, a ring to which a strap can be attached for balancing when standing up and loops on both sides for cossack fashion, hanging exercises. There are a number of basic exercises for which teams of 8 receive marks. This is usually followed by a free-style event.

Vaulting is fun and popular both with the young and with their teachers, for it is an excellent education. This combination of gymnastics, ballet and riding mean the children develop confidence, courage, rhythm, balance, grace and a feeling for the movements of the horse. It is also a good introduction to competitions and especially beneficial as the emphasis is on team rather than individual success.

Even in this sphere of riding it is the Germans who are the most consistent winners in Europe. It seems that in every age bracket, in every form of equestrian activities, the Germans are able to challenge the best in the world.

CHAPTER THREE

SWEDEN

TUCKED away in the north of Europe is the country whose riders have quietly accumulated more Olympic gold medals for dressage, show jumping and eventing, than any other country. They were won by a very small group of the people of Sweden – the cavalry – who monopolised equestrian activities for more than a century. The sporting country riders that were the backbone of English sport never featured in this Scandinavian nation.

The Swedish cavalry achieved their success through an enterprising and unprejudiced approach to riding. Their young officers were sent out to the great riding schools of Europe and they returned to adopt and to teach, not the French school, nor the German, or the Italian, or the Austrian, but a school which contained some of the best of all these methods. They were given Swedish warmblood horses to ride which were, again, the product of an enterprising compromise, as this breed has strains of German, English, Irish and Scandinavian blood. The result was that the Swedish cavalry dominated all types of equestrian events in the inter-war years, and were prominent in the post Second World War era.

After the Second World War, although the mechanisation of armies meant the gradual disbandment of the Swedish cavalry, officers still won medals. At the 1952 and 1956 Olympic Games, St. Cyr led two Swedish teams to victory in the dressage, and on both occasions was the individual champion himself. Hans von Blixen Finecke and Petrus Kastenman both won individual gold medals in the three-day events at the 1952 and 1956 Olympics respectively. By the end of the 1950s, however, there were few cavalrymen left and Sweden had to turn to civilians to find her competitors.

Equestrian activities became very amateurish affairs, which, although pleasant, yielded disappointing competitive results. The problem was that Sweden was a socialist country, in which there were no rich to support equestrian sport and where no government encouragement was forthcoming for what was considered a 'capitalistic' sport. The outcome was that civilian riders had neither the time, nor money, to give their riding the devotion needed for good results.

The 1960s might have been a bleak period in Sweden's equestrian history in terms of competitive results, but the government were converted to the benefits of horse sports. They were made aware of the excellence of riding as a character builder and that the risk element helps young people to get rid of pent up frustrations sportingly rather than violently in demonstrations, riots and muggings. They started to give financial and administrative aid to riding schools to encourage the young. Riding was taken up by increasing numbers of people and by the 1970s civilians had begun to make their mark in international events. Their first major achievement was when the three ladies, Ulla Håkanson, Ninna Swaab and Maud von Rosen won the team dressage bronze medal at the 1972 Munich Olympic Games.

Swedish riders today will have difficulty in rivalling the successes of the cavalry of that bygone era. They have to face stiffer opposition, nor do they have the time, finance or discipline that the cavalry enjoyed. But they do have assets. Nowadays Sweden's horses and many of her riding schools are the envy of the world.

THE HORSE

The Swedish horse is probably the country's greatest equestrian asset. Whilst other countries have scoured Ireland, England, Germany and France to find their Olympic horses, Sweden has, since the Second World War, won 6 gold medals on homebreds.

The ability of the Swedish horse has now been generally recognised, and today more than one-third of Sweden's 3-year-old geldings are being taken out of the country to help the Germans, the Swiss and the Danes win their medals. Even the Germans, with their exceptional movers, the Holsteins and the Hanoverians to draw from, are turning more and more to Sweden for dressage horses. Indeed, Piaff, winner of the individual dressage gold medal for Germany at the 1972 Olympic Games, is such an import. The movement of the German horse is, perhaps, the equal of the Swedish horse, but it is the intelligent temperament of the latter which makes it such an outstanding dressage horse. This is not their only successful trait however, for they have won gold medals in eventing too. Show jumping is the only equestrian activity in which the Swedish horse has not won any of the post Second World War Olympic gold medals.

Outstanding temperament is immediately apparent in the Swedish warmblood. The feature common to nearly all, are large, generous, alert eyes set far apart. One can see that they have neither the nervousness of the thoroughbred, necessitating tactful handling, nor the strong mindedness of the German breeds, requiring discipline.

The conformation of the Swedish warmblood, apart from the eyes as previously mentioned, is not so consistent. They tend to vary, in size from about 15 hands to 17 hands, in weight carrying capacity from lightweight to light-heavyweight. However, most tend to have an athletic, wiry shape and an eye-catching extended trot. Their only common deficiency is a narrow foot, but the Swedes claim this is not a cause of lameness and they also say that it makes the horse less cumbersome.

The Swedes are able to consistently breed athletic, intelligent, attractive horses because of the practical way they approach matters. They have been quick to realise that warmblood breeding could be tackled in much the same way as is thoroughbred breeding, and that the warmblood can be a breed in its own right. Consequently, they decided what characteristics they required of their breed, then obtained them, through matings determined on performance and on pedigree of parents and ancestors.

The cavalry had for hundreds of years monopolised riding in Sweden and consequently the warmblood was produced to meet their specific requirements. They wanted horses that would go across rough country in the extremes of Swedish weather. They needed, too, a horse that would accept a lack of expertise in the soldiers they would have to carry. Thus, stamina, endurance and good temperament were emphasised, and when, in the nineteenth century, sports became a feature of cavalry activities, athletic ability was added to breeding aims.

It was in the sixteenth century that the Swedes' demand for horses began to increase. Their native ponies are strong, high spirited animals, with endless stamina, but they lacked size, so Friesian stallions were imported from the Netherlands. The cross did not produce the lighter weight riding horse, so, during the seventeenth century there was an increase in imports from the Orient, Spain and England. Royalty became interested, and in 1621 a stud was set up in the grounds of the King's castle at Strömsholm. In 1658 a second major stud was created, at Flyinge in Skåne, in the southern part of Sweden. These two studs, Strömsholm and Flyinge became, and still are, the equestrian centres of Sweden.

During the eighteenth century these two studs were not able to supply enough horses for cavalry needs. Further importation became necessary, but it was done hastily and without thought of pedigrees. The government stepped in and took the first major steps towards establishment of a breed, when in 1874 they began one of the earliest warmblood stud books. Veterinary examinations were held too, for stallions and mares, after which the unsound, and those lacking pedigrees, were discarded and the best given prizes.

Importation was continued, but with more thought. The crossing of extremes was found to be unsuccessful. Instead of putting the British thoroughbred to the native Swedish pony, the Hanoverian and Trakehner were imported and used for intermediary crossing. This importation of German blood was a great success, and a large quantity was brought into the country. By 1923, of the government's 132 stallions, 40 were Hanoverian and 8 Trakehners. Eventually, enough of the Swedish warmbloods showed the qualities required, and by 1952 only 3 Hanoverians were amongst the 140 government stallions.

In common with, but perhaps more marked than in the rest of the world, the late 1940s and 1950s saw a decline of horse population in Sweden. Tractors and tanks took over much of the work formerly done by hroses. Cavalry regiments were disbanded. Horse demand fell, to such a degree that some government stallions served as few as four mares. It was decided to close the Strömsholm stud. A ruthless culling of the stallions was made and this turned out to be of benefit to the general standard of the breed.

Today every effort is being made to maintain this quality in the face of an increasing demand for horses.

This high general standard is not luck, it is the result of careful planning and hard work. Potential stallions are either bred at Flyinge, or bought as yearlings from farmers, and sometimes a thoroughbred or Hanoverian is imported. Young stock are given special feeding, and constant attention is paid to them so that bad feeders and ill-tempered ones can be noted and gelded. At 2½ years they are broken in and at 3 years they are ridden.

In the autumn of their third year comes their major trial. On the testing day they have to complete a road walk of between 12 and 15 kilometres at a minimum speed of 240 metres per minute, followed by a 3.5 kilometre cross-country course of 14 obstacles at a maximum height of 1 metre and 2 metres wide, where a minimum speed of 450 metres per minute must be maintained. Finally they have a flat race of 1,200 metres which they must run at more than 700 metres per minute. On completion they are subjected to a veterinary examination. Those who do not pass this rigid test of stamina, soundness and temperament are not allowed to breed. For those who do there is still one more hurdle. They stand at 3 years of age and are not given a final 'all clear' until their foals have been examined. The privileged, whose progeny will become members of the Swedish warmblood breed, are owned mostly by the government and live at Flyinge. Only a few private owners stand stallions on their own studs.

At Flyinge, during the winter, the stallions are ridden or driven every day. There is an indoor school, a covered ride, and a sanded courtyard where the horses can be trained to increasingly advanced work. It is the policy of the stud to continually test and prove the stallions' soundness and ability. One of their most famous stallions, Gaspari (sire of gold medal winner Piaff), took part in the Olympic dressage events both in Rome and Tokyo. Nowadays, however, stallions do not compete because 'their work here is more valuable' says the stud director, Mr. Kjellander. Nonetheless, all the stallions are schooled to test their ability. I saw Emir, an eye-catching 5-year-old chestnut (a son of Gaspari) performing the passage. But the stud can be tempted to sell and this potential dressage star was bought by the German rider, and owner of Piaff, Liselott Linsenhoff. I also saw Imer, the old grey stallion who had sired many international dressage stars, stand on his hind legs in his stable at the command of the stud director.

At an annual show in September, the capabilities of all these stallions are shown to the general public. In the sanded courtyard, in front of the director's old house, and in the enclosed grass arena, the stallions can be seen carrying out Grand Prix dressage movements, musical rides and being driven in carriages.

This display proves the excellence of the Swedish warmbloods' temperament, which is unusually intelligent and sensible. It is seen, too, in the stables of the National Stud. Most of the stallions are tied up in stalls, but those in stables are groomed loose. Visitors and workers wander in and out of the stables all the time, and there is no sign of bared teeth or nervousness. Mr. Kjellander shows off his stallions loose in their stables. Visitors crowd in and with his stick he gently pokes them into a position where they are standing well.

Looking after the stallions, under the supervision of government employed stud grooms, are school age trainee grooms. Some of them are only at the National Stud for a two-week course. They come on a government scheme to allow those nearing school leaving age to try out possible occupations. Consequently the stud gains labour and the school leavers can see if it would be a suitable career.

During the season groups of stallions are sent to different parts of Sweden to cover local mares, but the majority still remain at Flyinge. The work given to each stallion varies according to its age, but one popular fellow was said to have covered 140 mares!

Flyinge stands 42 Swedish warmblood stallions. With them are 4 thoroughbred stallions which are used to produce race-horses and to cross, when thought beneficial, with Swedish warmblood mares. The stud also houses a few mares, but the majority are owned by small farmers and private studs.

A systematic breeding programme has made the Swedish warmblood a very valuable product. Breeders can sell good colts to the government stud as stallions and they can send 3-year-old geldings to the regional Remontuppköps, or to the major sales at Jonköping in the summer and at Flyinge in September. Avelsforeningen – the Swedish Association for warmblood horses (an adjunct of their Ministry of Agriculture) organises these sales, as well as the May sale for 3-year-old fillies at Flyinge. The Association has been a good promoter of the breed for about one-third of the country's youngsters are exported, mainly to Denmark, Finland, Norway, Switzerland and Germany.

The Swiss have been the major importers of Swedish horses. They have bought close to 2,000 since the end of the Second World War. Their great dressage rider, Chammartin, achieved most of his successes on Swedish horses. Of late, it is the Germans who are moving in on the market, and the arrival of these determined buyers has pushed prices high. Although the Swedes are finding it difficult not to sell their most promising horses, the high-class horses exported are usually geldings because the Swedish government, one of the first to use its power to control breeding, are not going to let their warmblood breed deteriorate now. With this in mind mares and fillies are retained, and the cream of the yearlings are offered first to Flyinge.

RIDING CLUBS AND CENTRES

Apart from the Swedish warmblood horse, the Swedes have another great asset – their riding facilities. Indeed, and as is the case with most of Europe, these contrast with those available in Britain. In Sweden, the population is an urban one. Few Swedes own land on which to keep their horse. Then there is the weather. It is bitterly cold in winter and riding outside at times can be foolhardy. The result is that the riding club is used as a school for riding, stabling for the horses and is the basis of all equestrian activities. It also fulfils a social purpose, giving riding a community flavour, similar to such sports as football and hockey in the U.K.

At a typical club in Sweden some horses are privately owned, but the majority belong to the club, which is itself backed financially by the government. The reason for such state assistance is that increasing importance has been placed on equestrian education; riding being valued for the same reasons as in the courts of the seventeenth and eighteenth centuries, when it was considered an essential part of a young nobleman's education. Today the Swedish government claim 'Riding is a good and many-sided physical training, quite as valuable as most other branches of sport. It is able to further the moulding of character . . .' etc.

This approach has led to a membership of, primarily, teenagers who depend upon government financial aid to master riding. Indeed, instructors have to take a course in youth leadership so that they will be better equipped to handle their pupils.

Riding is regarded in Sweden as a means of broadening young people's education, rather than as a competitive sport which can gain prestige value for the country. Consequently, a high percentage of the population know how to ride, and may even have competed in shows during their teens. Few, however, continue serious riding when they grow too old for financial assistance from the government and, for most adults, riding becomes an occasional weekend 'jolly', or a memory of youth.

This tendency towards a transient riding population is not due to a lack of facilities. Sweden can boast of some of the best in the world, for it has become a prestige symbol for towns to have the biggest and best riding school. The taxpayer may suffer, but riders in such major cities as Malmö, Helsingborg and Gothenberg must be very grateful to be able to ride and compete under the superb conditions which are available there.

At Malmö there is a 68-metre indoor school with stabling for 60 horses. Designed with typical Scandinavian ingenuity, it is incorporated into the back of the grandstand at the racecourse. This school has become an especially comprehensive and active equestrian centre. The tracks for trotting, steeplechasing and flat racing are in regular use, and amongst these the dressage and show jumping horses have their outdoor facilities.

These centres in the major cities are modern and efficient. But at the national centre at Strömsholm, about a two-hour drive west of Stockholm, the Swedes can boast of tradition and beauty, in addition to facilities which surpass those of any other country. The centre is dominated by the seventeenth-century castle of Strömsholm, which has a natural moat surrounding it, formed by the river dividing around the island on which it stands.

On one side, this home of Swedish kings overlooks a permanent show jumping arena, containing fixed natural obstacles. Bordering the arena is a wide sand track and a small stand for spectators. Beyond the arena, between the river and the western shores of one of Sweden's largest lakes – Mälaren – are the meadows of Österängen. This is land for horsemen. The undulations and copses have formed many naturally protected areas which are ideal for schooling. A wide variety of small permanent obstacles mean that flat work can be enlivened with the odd leap into the air, but the central feature of these meadows is the high and wide brush fences which make up the course for the Swedish Grand National. The track for this event which attracts an international field wends its way between copses of birch trees, tall pines, 700-year-old oak trees and the shores of the lake. The Grand National takes place in the early summer and vast crowds flock to watch an exciting event in this glorious setting.

On the other side of the castle a narrow track runs through an avenue of trees. On either side there are fields, with some paddocks for grazing horses, but everywhere it is possible to train.

For hundreds of years the directors of Strömsholm have been intent on providing an abundance of stimulating and picturesque facilities for horse and rider. They have been successful, and this must be the most difficult place at which to get bored, and the easiest to envy. Horses can be trained in half passes along sandy tracks through woods, do their flying changes in corners near the river and their pirouettes in another area beside the castle.

The track from the castle leads to further facilities. The earliest of these dates back to 1621 when Swedish royalty took the first steps towards establishing this riding mecca, but it was not until 1868 that the army moved in, to turn Strömsholm into an equestrian school. Indoor dressage extravaganzas were the fashion in those days and a large elegant riding school with high arched windows was built.

In 1909 another indoor school was built alongside and this is decorated with the quotations of a nineteenth-century teacher at Strömsholm called Ehrengranath. He claimed that 'the true art of riding never grows old', and 'where art finishes, force starts'.

These two schools lie along one side of a large sandy courtyard which is used for schooling and the collection of rides. Two stable blocks and another indoor school line the remaining sides.

Such extensive indoor facilities are needed in this part of Sweden, as Strömsholm lies on the same latitude as Stockholm and the winters are severe. For part of the year those picturesque meadows lie beneath snow and ice, limiting outdoor activities to fun in the snow, and occasional races over the frozen lake of Mälaren.

Strömsholm caters for more than the training of horses and their riders. It has a high-class veterinary hospital, and it is typical of efficient Swedish organisation that similar hospitals with X-ray equipment, operating theatres, isolation units, stables and a group of veterinary surgeons are found in most of the major towns. However, Strömsholm, together with the Helsingborg and Stockholm Veterinary Hospitals, are the best known in Sweden.

The military created these unique equestrian facilities and they proved their worth, for Swedish cavalry officers won more Olympic medals than did any other army. During the inter-war period when they dominated equestrian competitions, cavalry recruits were given extraordinary opportunities to develop their riding talents. Instructors were sent on courses to the great schools of Europe. Those inclined towards jumping went to Pinerolo in Italy, and the others to Saumur in France, Hanover in Germany or to the Spanish Riding School in Austria. They returned unusually well qualified to teach and ride.

The training of cavalrymen at Strömsholm was broadly based. Everybody had to break in first year remounts, unlike most countries who left it to a specialised 'nagsman'. At Strömsholm they had to bring their second year remount up to elementary dressage level and to teach them to jump. They had to ride up to six horses a day and there was little specialisation. These six horses usually included a remount, a dressage horse, a jumper, an eventer, a steeplechaser and even horses for driving, as until 1968 it was the horse that took the guns through the woods. In the heyday of the cavalry, young officers could go steeplechasing one day and ride in a dressage class the next. They could go racing in the snow and draghunt during the winter. They could compete in every type of event in the summer. With Strömsholm castle for their residence, and an abundant supply of young and proven horses at their beck and call, the life of a Swedish cavalry officer must have been very good indeed.

After the Second World War, the social democratic principles of the government could not justify the expenditure on these activities. Strömsholm remained the army equestrian school, but remount depots and other schools were closed down. Horses were sold or sent to civilian riding schools. Cavalry regiments were disbanded until there was only one left out of the ten regiments active in the 1920s. At the present time there is just one small unit of Horse Guards, based in Stockholm, with 80 to 90 horses.

Strömsholm, after celebrating its centenary as a military riding academy, was abandoned by the cavalry in 1968. Unlike other famous European cavalry schools, such as Hanover, it was not closed down but was converted for the use of the new riders – the civilians. It became the National Riding Centre under the control of Ridfrämjandet.

Ridfrämjandet is a government financed association created to promote equestrian activity. It is one of a number of similar Swedish associations set up to promote healthy sports including skiing, bicycling and riding.

Ridfrämjandet draws up norms and standards for the 200 or so riding schools that come under its jurisdiction and is also responsible for the training and education of riding instructors and youth leaders. It is largely at Strömsholm that this is achieved. It is there that the instructors for the country's schools are trained and it is the chief instructor at Strömsholm who supervises and visits all of Sweden's riding schools.

The present chief instructor at Strömsholm is Major Hans Wikne who, as an ex-chief instructor at the military school, maintains a link with the past. The school has lost much of its glamour, there are no dashing officers in uniform showing off their ability, a commercial approach has put an end to many activities, and the horses are no longer likely to carry off gold medals. But it is still a unique school. The facilities are still there, and the horses (nearly one hundred) are the equal of, if not a higher standard than, those of any other European school. There are medium-class jumpers, many high-class dressage horses, one or two of which are capable of Olympic dressage movements. Students ride them every day and even compete on them in the ring.

Most of the students come to Strömsholm to take courses for instructors, and these prepare riders for two grades of qualification.

For the first grade the minimum qualifications are to have ridden for at least 5 years, to have taken part in two courses at Strömsholm the first of which lasts 8 weeks and the second 6 weeks, to have worked as an instructor for at least 2 years, to join a youth leadership course, to show suitability and good judgement and to be at least 21 years of age.

To become a second grade instructor the minimum qualifications are to have obtained the first grade, to work as an instructor for a further year, to take part in a longer youth leadership course, to be at least 23 years old and to take what is known as 'the long course' at Strömsholm.

Strömsholm's courses preparing students for Grade I qualifications are filled by Swedes starting their professional career with horses, but 'the long course' is open to foreigners. Usually, at least half of those on 'the long course' (about 12 students) come from other Scandinavian countries and some even from America. However, the small number of pupils that can be taught make it very difficult to be accepted. The students allowed to come, spend about 6 months at Strömsholm, where they are trained as competitors as well as instructors, taking part in dressage, events and jumping competitions. Their final test is at the show held in Strömsholm's beautiful permanent arena. Returning to normal riding establishments must seem very humdrum.

The school helps competitors, in addition to training professionals. Specialised courses are held in show jumping and dressage. Individual instruction can be arranged for riders with their own horses, and grooms too have their own courses. These courses are filled in the main by Swedes, and it is only 'the long course' that attracts foreigners in any numbers.

The students on the various courses serve the school too. Those on the short course for the first grade instructors break in young horses supplied by the army and the Swedish warmblood Association (Avelsforeningen). This takes place in the summer, and the 3-year-olds are kept out in the grass paddocks so that they do not get too obstreperous for their young riders. The more proficient pupils, on 'the long course', continue the training of these green horses. Under the watchful eye of the instructors both horse and rider learn and the expense of a professional breaker-in is avoided. Consequently the students are used to bring on the school horses for future pupils, and the instructors keep their hand in by taking over, and training the horses for the more advanced work. It seems the pattern is set to maintain a continuous supply of trained horses at Strömsholm.

THE TRAINERS

As we have seen, so far as her horses and riding facilities are concerned Sweden has assets to rival those of any country's. It is when we consider who makes use of them that weaknesses appear. The young trainers at Swedish establishments are rarely of an exceptional standard. The courses for Grade I and II instructors place great emphasis on youth leadership and less emphasis on equestrian ability. The qualifications demanded are not so rigorous as, for example, those in Germany and Denmark. The result is that Sweden has many efficient, workmanlike instructors who can mass produce a good standard of rider. But, no person who has been trained and has qualified under this system, has yet won repute as a trainer at international level.

The instructor's courses are not the only source of trainers. There are many ex-cavalrymen available who possess an unrivalled equestrian education. Indeed, many of the top equestrian posts, especially in administration, are held by gentlemen with military titles. Many, however, have left the system, as the transition to train civilians, as in Switzerland, has been too difficult. They were accustomed to teaching young men who had to take discipline, and who could practise on many horses. Today they have to cope with wayward teenagers and fewer horses.

Major Hans Wikne

The most important Swedish trainer, a product of the cavalry, is Major Hans Wikne, the national dressage and chief instructor at Strömsholm. He gained all his education and experience as a member of the Swedish cavalry. He was the chief rider for the cavalry in the 1950s and was a member of the Swedish dressage team in two Olympic Games. Major Wikne faithfully adheres to the principles and the methods of the Swedish cavalry. It is reassuring that this successful approach is being passed on to young civilian riders. At the same time he has been aware, when applying these principles, of the differences between soldier recruits and civilian pupils. Happily he has been broadminded enough to adapt to the circumstances of the present day where Swedish riders are predominantly amateurs. They ride for fun after work and cannot be expected to devote the same amount of time, nor be subjected to as much discipline, as were the cavalrymen.

Major Wikne's talent for adapting to circumstances proved invaluable during the training of the Swedish 1972 Olympic Games dressage team. Three ladies were chosen as the possible riders. One, Ulla Håkanson lived quite conveniently in Stockholm and Major Wikne was able to train with her once a month. The second, Maud van Rosen, lived in Skåne, in the south, so he limited that 6-hour journey to training sessions every 2 months. However, the most difficult case of all was that of Ninna Swaab who had married the Dutch dressage rider, J. M. Swaab, and had moved to Holland. Ninna Swaab could have no individual lessons, and only came on the 2 courses held at Strömsholm for potential Olympic riders. Major Wikne accepting the individual needs of each of these riders and adapting his training of them accordingly, was able to put together a team of ladies who carried off the Olympic dressage team bronze medal.

The aim of Major Wikne's teaching is to get horse and rider in harmony. To achieve this the horse must be well balanced, with a good outline and going between hands and legs; and the rider must sit correctly. A good seat not only looks more attractive but, more important, it is only from the correct position that the aids can be accurately applied.

The English hunting seat might be effective for that sport where absolute control is not necessary; but it is not the most natural and if the English riders were to spend hours without stirrups, as the pupils do at Strömsholm, they would find themselves slipping into a different position.

With the correct seat the rider can apply clearer aids, which makes it easier to get the horse going in the best possible manner. The first aim is to get the horse 'on the bit'. This is a feature of the Swedish way of riding, where from the early stages of training the horse is asked to go forward always accepting the bit and with submissiveness throughout. The idea of riding a young horse

---

Page 112 - SWEDEN

on a loose rein or with little contact is rarely practised in Sweden.

At Strömsholm, they like to give the horse a great deal of outdoor work, so that they can have the stimulation of fresh scenery and also learn to balance themselves on undulating ground. It is a feature of the Swedish school to favour riding outdoors whenever possible. However, this is done in a different way to that of England, where most riders simply hack across country. The Swedes like to introduce exercises, turns on the forehand, circles, changes of pace – all done to develop suppleness and an easy, smooth contact with the bit. I saw for myself when I was at Strömsholm a young lady on an eye-catching grey, spend part of her ride, going in half-pass from one side of the wide sandy track to the other, and another rider doing 'shoulder-in' along a narrow wooded track.

For a year or more the horses at Strömsholm receive the same basic training. However, if it is decided that they should concentrate on jumping, then the movements practised on the flat are those that promote suppleness and balance. Show jumpers spend much of their time doing turns on the forehand, leg yielding, backing, small circles, counter canter, but movements designed to develop the maximum possible collection, required of a dressage horse, are avoided.

Major Hans Wikne is the most important voice in choosing the Swedish riders who the government will help to give further training, from the novice to the Olympic level. He looks for two things in a rider to warrant this training: a good seat, and good 'feel'. 'Feel' he describes as enabling the rider to know what to do at the right moment, to be able to give the appropriate aids at this right moment and even to feel what is going to happen before it does. Without this instinct, Wikne says, no one can be a top rider; the greatest riders he says are born with it, but experience and hard work can develop it.

Major Boltenstern

One who was born with this ability to 'feel' is Major Boltenstern, who was the head instructor at Strömsholm before Major Wikne. He was not only one of the greatest Swedish dressage riders, but also one of the most popular. He has healthy Swedish good looks and eyes that twinkle, especially when making one of his

PLATE 12
Pupils and trainers gathered in front of Strömsholm castle.

PLATE 13
The director's house at Flyinge with Emir, the son of Gaspari, at exercise in the courtyard.

PLATE 14 (*above*) Swedish warmblood mares waiting for their feed at Flyinge.

PLATE 15 (*right*) A team of Swedish warmbloods being driven in the courtyard at Strömsholm.

frequent humorous asides. He is old now and uses a walking stick, but enjoys watching pupils perform.

Boltenstern rode in three Olympic dressage teams, two of which won gold medals, and on the third occasion he himself won the individual bronze. He joined the cavalry in its heyday, and he left as it was heading towards virtual extinction. His last post at the Remount Depot ended with the horses being taken away to supply riding schools.

It is surprising that Sweden did not make more use of this great rider's ability as a trainer. He has helped odd individuals, but it is a British family, the Sivewrights of Gloucestershire, who have benefited most from his tuition since his retirement from the army. His bi-annual trips have helped them to play a major role in British dressage.

Major Boltenstern's methods are especially suited to the temperament of the British thoroughbred. He is a devotee of the French school, possibly due to a year he spent studying at Saumur in the early 1930s. His horses respond to very light aids and his pupils are advised to develop the harmony of the horse, through winning the horse's co-operation rather than by relying on brute force. The least improvement, or one movement well done and Boltenstern is delighted. The horse is rewarded, the pupil praised, and often they are told 'that is enough'. He avoids the hours and hours of training practised by those schools who are more discipline orientated, such as the Germans.

Boltenstern is a great protagonist of dressage, believing that it helps everything. He related to me an anecdote, as an example of his belief. A steeplechaser, which he had been lent for the winter, had disappointed its owner with persistent failure on the race-track. Boltenstern did not enjoy riding this stiff untrained horse and soon taught him some dressage movements. After a winter spent in suppling exercises the horse was transformed and made a successful return to racing the following spring.

Stig Claesson

In the south of Sweden at Helsingborg, one of Major Bolten-stern's cavalry recruits, Stig Claesson, is building up his own training establishment. When he left the army, he joined the mounted police and there surprised his superiors when he trained one ordinary police horse after another up to Prix St. George standard. Unfortunately, he did not have the capital to start his own equestrian centre, but he did continue to keep and train horses at Malmö Riding School. He, and his wife, Maj, used to get up at 2.30 a.m. to ride their six horses before starting work at 8 a.m. 'If you like horses, that is the sort of thing you do', was his wife's only comment to that existence!

Eventually, they accumulated enough capital from selling trained dressage horses, to acquire an old cattle barn outside Helsingborg. In 1968 they started the work which turned this into an effective training unit. With hardly any outside help the couple built 15 loose boxes in part of the barn, and put down peat in the remaining section to make a small indoor school. Outside, using sand washed off the local farmer's sugar beet, they laid out a full-size dressage arena, and another, larger area of grass was fenced off. In this way they achieved the independence which is so rare for a Swedish trainer.

The Claessons now train horses and riders as a full-time occupation. Maj, who used to show jump, breaks in the youngsters, then hands them over to Stig after about two years. Some are sold to Germany, Silver Dream, who became one of the top dressage horses in Europe, was one such horse. Others are bought to be kept in the yard and there are normally one or two trained horses on which capable students can get the feel of the most difficult movements.

Being a small unit the lessons are individual, and adapted according to the needs of each pupil, making the approach towards training very different to that at Strömsholm. The objectives differ too, for whereas Strömsholm concentrates on the more long term aim of getting horse and rider to go in a classical manner, the Claessons are more concerned with quick results. To stay in business they need to win competitions and to give their students the greatest possible experience of more advanced work. The time spent perfecting basic principles is condensed, in order to reach the higher echelons of dressage as quickly as possible.

Without government finance, and with only a small indoor riding arena, the Claessons give full rein to the Swedish preference for using nature as a training aid. On every possible day they are outside on the sand, or on the grass arenas, or in the woods. During my own stay I faced autumn gales and sunshine and there is no doubt that it adds great stimulation and hardiness to the horses.

Stig Claesson likes to train the rider by he himself schooling the horse which would then give the pupil the correct feel. He also preferred to demonstrate on horseback, rather than by lengthy verbal description.

The first demonstration I received, was how to ride leg yielding. Claesson demonstrated on horseback. He loves his riding and he extended his demonstration a little further. He completed barely more than half a dozen strides in a straight line as he was continually asking his horse for some different exercise. The horse could hardly get bored, for he was always changing activities. He was either going sideways, changing pace, halting, turning on the haunches or the forehand. It was hard but stimulating work, which ended with Claesson doing flying changes at every stride on his 7-year-old Swedish horse.

The demonstration completed, it was now the turn of us pupils. Claesson was keen that his students should get the 'feel' of the more difficult movements. Nor was this an occasional treat, for he asked me to perform different and demanding movements in quick succession. It was exhausting to be continuously applying and changing aids, especially as the Claessons rarely let their horses relax and stretch their necks. They believe that the work should be short and hard.

A final exercise with the advanced horse was performed alongside the fence. I was told to hold my legs back and to apply them with rhythmical nudges. Simultaneously, I was to give the same rhythmical pressures on the reins. My tutor walked alongside with a long stick, tapping the horse's hind legs gently, and making regular clicking noises. Suddenly the suspension of the trot became longer, and we were doing the passage!

Stig Claesson starts preparing his horses for passage and piaff at 5 years. With his wife as rider, applying the correct aids, he remains on the ground using his long stick to gently tap the horse's hind legs. The horse soon learns to raise the tapped hind legs higher, initially helping to make the hind legs more active and ultimately becoming the passage.

After half to three-quarters of an hour, training sessions were generally rounded off with a walk in the nearby woods, where both horse and rider could relax along undulating tracks winding through the pines and silver birches.

Students do not only ride trained horses. Schooling a young horse is basic to dressage riding. I rode a bronze 3-year-old chestnut to gain this experience and was quite dumbfounded when, in my first lesson, I was told to do some leg yielding, turns on the haunches, shoulder-in and even a flying change.

Later Claesson told me about his unusually demanding approach to training young horses. He likes to get them working quickly and in a variety of movements. This helps to supple them up and to keep them interested. Naturally the youngsters do not do the movements with much precision, or collection, as to do otherwise, at this stage, would be asking too much and might strain and sicken them. The purpose is to acquaint the young horses with the idea of the movements, to keep the horse's interest through the variety of going sideways, stopping and turning, and so on. It is surprising how well Claesson succeeds in this.

Making the horse work without causing it discomfort, rests on obtaining co-operation and avoiding damaging battles. The Claessons' approach to this is by using an extraordinarily friendly approach. They spend a considerable time with the horses in the stables treating them more like dogs. The horses respond by following the Claessons around. The horses are never tied up and receive many titbits. However, one bite, or kick, or show of disobedience, and they are reprimanded with the voice and hand. The aim is to make them trusting but obedient. The horse 'must be right inside the head, before we do anything with him', Maj Claesson told me. When I was there one wilful 3-year-old had not been ridden as yet and was being lunged for his fourth month. The Claessons had not got him 'right inside the head' and therefore riding would have to wait. They wanted to avoid fights and battles.

In order to prevent a fight the Claessons are not beyond using gadgets. Most of their young horses are ridden in running martingales to stop them throwing their heads too high. Perhaps this acceptance of the benefits of some gadgets comes from Maj Claesson's experience of training show jumpers.

On the Continent the approach to jumping and to dressage is remarkably similar. Maj Claesson believes in training jumpers up to medium dressage standard, with all performing half-passes, turns on the haunches and shoulder-in. She tries to obtain some collection but always keeps in mind that, for the jumpers, forward impulsion is most important. The aim of these movements is to make the horse loose and obedient, not to win dressage tests. Accuracy and collection are not important for jumpers.

To support her belief in the importance of dressage for jumpers, she recalled the time Fritz Thiedemann, a member of the German Olympic show jumping team in 1952, 1956 and 1960, went through most of the Grand Prix movements on his famous horse, Meteor, before entering the ring for a jumping class. He might not have earned good marks for this dressage warm-up, but he was using them as a suppling exercise. The benefits of this training are supported by Meteor's exceptionally long life span as a top show jumper. He achieved one individual bronze in the 1952 Olympics and two team gold medals in 1956 and 1960 before he retired.

Dressage education for jumpers would appear to be beneficial. The Swedish horse, Ajax, was good enough to be Scandinavian champion jumper before he decided he no longer liked the sport, and refused to take on the larger fences. His owner tried dressage and within a few years won a team bronze medal at the 1972 Olympics. Talisman was one of the best jumpers in Denmark before he, too, decided he preferred to stay on the ground. After a few years training however, he won the highest Danish placing in the Munich Olympic Games dressage.

As a means to finding the capital to set up and expand their own equestrian centre, the Claessons bought some 2- or 3-year-olds and trained them on to sell. A profitable turnover proved that they had a good 'eye' for a horse and they told me about what they looked for. When buying, the first thing they considered was the action, although they do believe that weakness in the paces can be overcome to some degree, as long as the conformation is good.

To the Claessons, one of the best indicators of the possibility of a good extended trot being achieved by a horse, is the length of its cannon bone. As long as this is short and, more especially, shorter than the forearm, then training should bring out this all important movement. A wide front is necessary to help the horse carry out lateral movements. If the front is too narrow then it is difficult for the horse to cross its legs. The length of the hind cannon should not be too long. If it is, then the hind leg tends to move out and upwards instead of forwards. When looking at the shape of the hind leg, if an imaginary straight line is drawn down through the leg, then the hoof should not fall either side. If the hind leg is too straight, that is to say the hoof is behind the line, then the horse's action will lack suppleness, and if the hock is too bent then it is a sign of weakness.

Temperament is very important, and it is the eye that is the best indication to temperament. The eye must have a kind look, not suspicious, but open, frank, confident, fearless, inquisitive and alert, then the horse should do his work willingly. When a horse shows these characteristics the Claessons are not too worried about white around the eye. But they are worried about shy or nervous horses. 'They need to have a little bit of "hallo", for dressage', said Maj Claesson.

The rider should be something of a psychoanalyst, in order to understand his horse's temperament and to know when to reward, and when to punish. He must have great patience, and, the most elusive quality of all, 'feel'. As Major Wikne has observed, 'feel' can be developed, although it is a natural instinct basically. It is essential in a top-class rider so he will know what is right, and what is wrong, even before the horse does it. Correct application of reward, or punishment, will then ensue, and the horse will better understand what is required of him. Claesson gave me examples of riders who he believes have this 'feel', the two Swedish riders, Nyblaeus and Boltenstern.

Depending on nationality, riders use their 'feel' in various ways. The Germans obtain results in a very different way from the Swedish, according to Claesson. His views are notable, because he has sold many horses to Germany, and spends a good deal of his time there. He said that the German riders are usually harder, their horses are more compressed and that they do not move so freely. Horses in the hands of Germans are developed quicker, and reach Grand Prix standard before those in Sweden.

However, Germans are multi-horse riders and they can afford

to have write-offs. The Swedes rarely have more than two horses, and they take great care of their animals. Their horses are not allowed to start competition work until they are 5-year-olds.

Stig Claesson thought another characteristic of the Swedish approach is the importance attached to keeping a horse on the bit. It was notable that Claesson's horses worked best with a stronger tension on the reins than those I rode elsewhere. The Swedes, he said, do not like to get their horses long and low like the French and British, for they think this makes it difficult for the horses to use their hind legs correctly. He thought, also, that the Swedes were not nearly so demanding of their horses as the Germans. The Germans take more 'will' out of their horses. For him the horse must know when to obey, but must not be dead and sorrowful. Like a child, they must understand discipline, but without suppressing the character.

Stig and Maj Claesson could never produce anything that was dead and sorrowful. Their whole life is the horse. They have defied conventions in social democratic Sweden and have worked to their utmost in order to lead an individual life. They have adopted speedy methods to get quick results, and this is not typical of all Swedes, but pupils can gain much from them. Their sacrifice for independence is an indication of a thoughtful, determined, adaptable and enthusiastic approach to life and this they have also applied to riding.

Jan Olof Wannius

Today, dressage is Sweden's most successful equestrian medium, but there are more participants in show jumping. As in most countries, except Germany and neighbouring Denmark, dressage tends to attract the more mature rider. In Sweden, most riders are teenagers. They want to jump and they can be trained to do so, at the riding clubs.

The most outstanding trainer at a riding club is the young professional, Jan Olof Wannius. He manages the luxurious riding school in Malmö, and is Sweden's most successful show jumper. He has been the national champion for a number of years, though his popularity as a trainer gives him little time these days to compete abroad. Some years ago, however, he proved his worth in international circles, becoming the only Swedish rider

since the Second World War to have won a major competition
in Britain. He won the *Daily Telegraph* Cup at the Horse of the
Year Show in 1969.

Åke Hultberg

The most serious opposition in competitions to Wannius, comes
from two young men, Hultberg and Nätterquist. Åke Hultberg
has had the greatest successes internationally, with his two horses,
Magnor and El-Vis. He now manages the Helsingborg riding
club, but his family home is also a renowned training and equestrian centre. Hultberg's father was a military instructor at
Strömsholm and nowadays runs a stud farm. He began teaching
at the farm, Åke being one of his first pupils; his popularity
grew and now a large number of aspiring riders come to him
for assistance.

Ted Nätterquist

The second challenger to Wannius also has a famous father.
A talented trainer, Nätterquist senior was also Sweden's best
show jumper in the 1960s. He trained, and eventually sold to
England, in the first part of this decade, Grey Friar. This horse
changed hands for the largest price ever paid at that time; but
with Ted Williams as his new rider Grey Friar never did produce
the sort of results in England, which he had in Sweden. Nätterquist
holds courses for young show jumpers, but his star pupil is his
son, Ted, who has become a good enough rider to represent
Sweden at many European events. Ted Nätterquist rode for
Sweden in the World Championships, held at Hickstead in 1974.
He has now chosen training as a career, and has been gaining
experience abroad, spending time with Nelson Pessoa in France,
and with Fergus Graham in Britain.

Göran Casparsson

Sweden's national trainer of show jumpers is Göran
Casparsson and his base, like the national dressage trainer's,
is at Strömsholm. Casparsson was trained at Strömsholm as a
civilian, when it was still a military establishment. He was ear-
marked as an outstanding pupil and given a subsidy by Ridfrämjandet. With this help he established himself quickly as a high-

grade trainer. Today he is responsible for all the jumping training at Strömsholm and frequently travels to give short courses.

Colonel Nyblaeus

Young trainers are now in exalted positions in Swedish show
jumping, which has led to a more up-to-date and international
approach to training. However, a limited number of shows at
which to gain experience, and a lack of high prize money to
encourage a more professional approach, leaves show jumping
behind dressage as the sport in which Sweden earns most international respect.

The Swede with the greatest international reputation is Colonel
Gustaf Nyblaeus. He is an Olympic judge and President of the
F.E.I. dressage committee. In these various roles he becomes a
great influence on the techniques of riding, for he makes rules,
creates tests, and makes judgements on how the tests shall be
ridden.

With this power Colonel Nyblaeus holds a very controversial
position, but although a few disagree with some of his ideas, I
have heard of no one who does not respect and like him. He is a
free talker who is fired with enthusiasm about his work. After a
long discussion with me on one occasion he apologised, 'I talk
from the heart rather than the head' he said. But this spirit and
his genuine attitude has led to his high reputation.

Colonel Nyblaeus is now a jet set traveller, going to committee
meetings in one country, judging dressage in another, and a
three-day event in yet another. His background, however, is
that of a professional soldier. This was his family tradition, his
father having served in the cavalry at the end of the last century,
during which time he was made chief instructor at Strömsholm
in the 1880s. He encouraged those officers whose only equestrian
interest was dressage to start cross-country riding and steeplechasing. It was said 'he opened the doors of the riding school'.

Nyblaeus himself was sympathetic to his father's ideas, and
it was not until his later years when he became Commander at
Strömsholm that he concentrated on dressage rather than eventing.

It was during his term as Commander, in the 1950s, that his
present career developed. He could have become a trainer, but
as he says he 'fell into judging'. However, it would be more

accurate to say he was enticed into it by the many dressage organisers who realised his worth. His initiation as an international judge was at Aachen in 1954, and from that date he received an increasing number of invitations from all over the world. He accepts not only those for Grand Prix dressage competitions, but for university eventing championships, for the rural championships and even for show jumping at the Horse of the Year Show in Britain. It is part of his character to seek out various activities and to help all types and standards, not just the 'greats' of the dressage world.

Colonel Nyblaeus might think he fell into this career but it was with no reluctance. He knows that in dressage, unlike other equestrian activities, judges are as important as trainers.

Nyblaeus has clear views about the characteristics needed in order that a judge may exercise his influence beneficially. He listed for me what he thinks are the most important characteristics of a good judge:

(i) A strong personality which is fair, not overbearing or obstinate.

(ii) An ability to be generous and unbiased so as not to be affected by personalities or previous performances.

(iii) A quick eye which will give an accurate assessment of the whole picture, the general impression, and not just the details.

(iv) Judgements which can be made, bearing in mind that precision, which is so much easier to assess, is not the only maxim of dressage.

(v) A good memory so as to remember how earlier competitors did a movement and what mark they were given for it.

Colonel Nyblaeus also remarked, with a twinkle in his eye, that judges must have the strength to resist excessive food and alcohol before and during their work. Such pleasant diversions only lead to marred judgements and embarrassing snoozes! Having said what characteristics a judge should have, he added that he was not expecting to meet his perfect specimen although all should endeavour to reach it!

The qualities Nyblaeus asks for in a judge are demanding, but then judges are very powerful people. Unlike other equestrian sports, dressage demands that they make judgements. The competitors rely on them entirely to make a true and fair assessment of their horses training and to determine the result of the competition. They decide what qualities should be most highly rewarded (they have to decide upon the importance attached to precision, to suppleness or to impulsion) and, as such, they determine what the riders should aim for in their training. Every judge contributes, by his decisions, to the form dressage takes in his club, country or the world.

Colonel Nyblaeus feels that the present form of dressage could be improved. The surge in popularity of this sport has led to many participants lacking knowledge and there are not enough trainers to give it to them. Tests may be performed with geometric accuracy but this all too often leads to rigid mouths, stiff necks, tense backs and trudging quarters.

This is not a new development, more than two hundred years ago, the father of classical dressage, de la Guérinière, said, 'A horse which is not absolutely supple, loose and flexible, cannot conform to the will of man with ease and carriage. To our disgrace we must admit that the desire for the beautiful in this fine art has decreased a great deal in our time. Instead of, as was formerly the case, striving to gain the most difficult movements, which constitute the grace of the manège and shed lustre on reviews and ceremonies, one nowadays contents oneself with too careless practice.'

Reassuring as it might be to find we are not faced with a novel problem, there is still a great deal that the judges can do to improve today's approach towards dressage. They can show their disapproval of any poor form of dressage, and be consistent in rewarding combinations that display de la Guérinière's classical aims of dressage.

Colonel Nyblaeus has summarised what he wants the rider to aim for in a test. Firstly, he wants paces that display freedom and regularity. Secondly, impulsion, which is the desire to move forward with elasticity of the steps, suppleness of the back and engagement of the hindquarters. Thirdly, submission, which is a horse showing attention and confidence, harmony, lightness, ease of the movements and acceptance of the bridle with a light contact and submissiveness throughout.

Judges have another important role and that is as the major devisers of tests. The contents of them influence the aims of the rider so it is important, therefore, that the movements reward suppleness, looseness, flexibility, confidence and obedience. The tests, too, should be logically constructed, each test being gradually more and more demanding, neither too easy nor too severe for the level concerned, and asking for increasing collection. There is another aim to keep in mind when devising tests. They should be easy to judge, and therefore more likely to yield fair results. Nyblaeus thought it easier to give many marks in quick succession, each for a very small section of the test, rather than for one mark to cover a large number of movements.

Few would disagree with the aims of dressage tests, but the movements by which they are achieved are more controversial. Nyblaeus has found this out, for he caused a storm in the dressage world with the international tests he devised in 1972 for senior and junior three-day events and for the junior dressage championships. He introduced a movement which has not been included before in international tests, leg yielding. His own strong personality, a characteristic he called for in his perfect judge, was tested to the full. He was attacked and questioned both in America and Europe.

Leg yielding is one of the simplest lateral movements for the horse, moving sideways in response to the rider's inside leg aid, and slightly bent at the poll away from the direction of the movement. Leg yielding is not a new movement, for a description of it can be found in the Swedish, Danish and German riding manuals for the cavalry, written at the beginning of this century. In Scandinavia, Germany and Switzerland, it is part of daily riding routine, but dressage exponents in America, England and some of the lowland European countries have little time for it. Their representatives have put arguments to Nyblaeus and the international dressage committee calling for its immediate removal from international tests. Some feel it is only a training movement, others, that it is confusing for the horse when he is asked for more advanced lateral movements requiring a different bend. Colonel Nyblaeus believes he is right. He thinks leg yielding together, later on, with the more advanced movement of shoulder-in is the best means of making a horse supple, loose and unconstrained.

Nyblaeus will become part of dressage history as the 'leg

yielding protagonist', but he is well known too for his occasional controversial marks. He has stood up against fashion and the dressage stars, to make his own judgements. In the 1972 Olympics at Munich his mark for Neckermann, the host country's favourite was much lower than that of the other judges. Neckermann was relegated to third place because of Nyblaeus, which caused another storm. Few judges have the knowledge, or the strength of character, to do this. It is one of the controversial aspects of dressage, that lack of knowledge and not enough strength of mind on the part of the judges, leads to disputed results.

Some claim that the present supremacy of the Germans is due to the judges' excessive admiration of precision and fear of upsetting the establishment. Colonel Nyblaeus would disagree, as he believes that the Germans over the last few years have been the best followers of the *Objects and General Principles of Dressage* (as laid down in the F.E.I. rules).

Nor is the British riders' failure to achieve the higher placings in dressage competitions due to the judges' lack of appreciation of their style. Colonel Nyblaeus believes that the thoroughbred is not such a natural dressage horse as some of the Continental breeds. Although good at the walk and canter, in his view they lack freedom in their shoulders. This can restrict their extended trot. Often they have more difficult nervous temperaments and cannot take too much domination. However, he did add that there were exceptions.

He believes that British riders have a common weakness, because in tests and training they tend to fail to produce true extension or collection. The contrasts are not great enough, they are not daring enough. So many of the British competitors do not ride for extension, they tend to lengthen their reins too much and the horse just goes faster. What is required is an extended stride not an increase of speed. This is best achieved by the rider asking for a half-halt, before extending, holding the horse back and then pushing him forward, without giving with the hands in an exaggerated way.

Likewise British competitors do not ride for true collection. Often they ask for collection at a too early stage in the dressage tests and this is a mistake, for the horse should be supple before being collected. To get good collection the rider must work to increase the impulsion to ride forward, and then to decrease the length of the stride by pushing the horse into the hands with repeated half-halts. Collection must come from the hind legs being pushed under the horse's body rather than the reins holding him back. The horse must not just go slower but become more elevated. The lateral movements, travers, renvers and last, but not least, shoulder-in, can all be used to improve the collection if executed in the right way.

The British style is rarely daring enough. The horses need to be ridden forward more and the exercises built up so that the horse really listens to the rider. Developing this forward movement can be done in traditional English fashion. Colonel Nyblaeus did not encase his dressage horses in cotton wool and send them around enclosed arenas day after day. He took them hunting, jumping and hacking up and down hills. He believed that by changing their work, and riding them in different ways, they became more elastic and interested, attentive and confident.

It is likely that if Colonel Nyblaeus' career had gone another way, Sweden would have been boasting of a world famous trainer, rather than of a renowned judge.

ADMINISTRATION AND COMPETITION

For most Swedes riding is purely a healthy means of exercise especially beneficial to the young. It is dealt with in much the same way as other sports and rarely treated as a vocation, but this does not mean that Swedes do not go in for competitions. Shows are on the increase, with events most weekends. A hundred, or more, competitors do take part, but, with the odd exception, it is simply a demanding form of exercise for these riders. The competitive spirit, or an absorption in horses, has not been engendered by the riding clubs, where mass production and uniformity is all important.

One equestrian activity particularly well suited to the Swedes' approach towards riding, is run by the Rural Riders Federation. This is an annual European Championship open to farmers, breeders and their families. It is a most comprehensive test of a horse and rider. Participants have to jump, complete a dressage test, go across country and drive, all with the same horse. The restrictions on membership and the range of requirements means that there is little likelihood of professionalism creeping in.

The Swedes are major supporters of the Rural Riders Federation. Their national stud director – Kjellander – is the president. They held the European championships at Flyinge in 1973, and teams from Germany, Austria, Switzerland, Holland, Belgium and Denmark competed in this truly amateur equestrian activity.

Children, too, have an association which is organising an increasing number of competitions for them. The Svenska Ponnyforening runs events in which the emphasis is on serious riding. There are no gymkhana events, or other games on horse-back. It is in dressage and jumping that the ponies and their young riders are tested. There are international competitions of this kind, which attract teams from the neighbouring Scandinavian countries. And in 1972, a European championship for ponies in dressage and jumping was held at Flyinge.

Eventing is the one sport in which amateurs all over the world can still shine and it would seem a good activity for the Swedes. However there are only a small number of such events in Sweden. The well publicised injuries to horses and riders competing over the formidable Olympic cross-country course at the 1956 Stock-holm Games, shocked the Swedish public. Eventing became an 'out' sport but time is healing the wounds. Memories are short, and an increasing number of events are now held each year. Sweden, the old masters of eventing, earned their first success in nearly two decades at the Munich Olympics when J. Jonsson on Sarajevo carried off the individual bronze medal. Success generates enthusiasm and eventing is regaining supporters in Sweden.

Equestrian competitions in Sweden are controlled by Svenska Ridsporten Centralförbund. This association lays down the rules and pays out considerable sums towards transport costs for com-petitors and prize money at the major shows. It also helps to send riders abroad, and Swedish show jumpers are appearing at international events in increasing numbers.

Sweden's shows take place throughout the year, although during the winter they tend to be smaller, indoor, club events. The rewards are small. Sponsorship has only recently been intro-duced, and then only at a very few shows, and winners normally have to be content with silver trophies.

Small international shows are held at Helsingborg, Malmö and Strömsholm but the visiting competitors rarely come from other Scandinavian countries.

Faesterbö show held in the south was the first to provide good prize money. Their major competition, the Swedish Jumping Derby, carries with it a large prize, and the dressage events are relatively well financed. Since 1973 top jumping and dressage riders from Germany, England, and other Scandinavian countries have taken part. This introduction to Sweden of the glamour and excitement of international events has led to greater things.

In 1975 Vasternäs show (close to Stockholm) was held for the first time. It attracted the greatest jumping stars in the world. Sponsors paid out large sums in appearance money and high prizes. Hans Winkler, Alwin Schockemöhle, Hartwig Steenken, David Broome and Harvey Smith were among those who competed.

Such ventures as Vasteräs show must change the nature of equestrianism in Sweden. Although the vast majority of riders will keep the riding clubs prosperous, compete for fun and not take things too seriously, the growth of financial incentives to win, the stimulus of competing against and seeing some of the best riders in the world, must lead to some Swedish riders adopting a more professional and dedicated approach towards riding. If they prove to be as enterprising and broadminded as were earlier generations of Swedish riders – learning from all nations – then the prospects will be good and civilians are likely to add to that record number of Olympic Games gold medals won by Swedish cavalry officers.

Nina Swaab on Casanova. They were partners at the Olympic
Games in 1972, helping Sweden win the team bronze medal.

PLATE 17
Henri Chammartin performs passage on the Swedish warmblood
Wolfdietrich.

CHAPTER FOUR

SWITZERLAND

SWITZERLAND, like Sweden, is a neutral country and this has produced similarities. Swedes and Swiss tend to lead orderly, well planned and unostentatious lives. They display much good sense and although this can inhibit creativity, it does mean that they are sufficiently unprejudiced to adopt ideas that work elsewhere.

Both Switzerland and Sweden have studied other methods of riding and breeding, not applying one approach wholesale, but pruning out the ideas that suit them.

In other respects they differ, capitalism, not socialism, is the Swiss doctrine and private wealth is in abundance. Individualism is respected and preserved, leading to a race of highly competitive people.

Such characteristics do not end at the personal level. Switzerland was created by uniting states which now form cantons, each with its own local government. Achieving a consensus of opinion between the highly individual and independent cantons is similar to having to deal with the English, Irish and Welsh.

But there is a further, and even stronger, division in Switzerland and that is between the French, German and Italian speaking people. Their respective outlook and character, as well as their language, are different and each group exercises influence with the government, for Switzerland was one of the earliest countries to embrace, and remains a constant exponent of, democracy. Every Swiss has a right, which he does not fail to exercise, to express his or her views to any authority. All this applies to the horse world and a positive centralised general policy, designed to help equestrian competitors, has proved elusive.

One who has helped to overcome divergent interests and

methods to create a formidable show jumping team, has been their leading rider Paul Weier. In 1973 the Swiss were behind only Great Britain and Germany in the World team championship – the President's Cup. Also Paul Weier carried off the individual honour of a victory in the 1973 Aachen Grand Prix. The success of the adults has been backed up by the juniors, Switzerland having won the 1970 and 1972 individual junior European championships and the 1973 and 1976 team championships.

The achievements of the show jumpers compensated the Swiss for a bleak period in dressage. In the 1950s and early 1960s the Swiss cavalry officers consistently won medals in the team championships. Their stars, Gustav Fischer and Henri Chammartin, gained individual silver and gold medals in the Olympics and World championships. Then with the dissolution of the cavalry, no civilians were able to achieve this standard. The Swiss earned no international honours until 1974 when a young lady, Fraulein Stückelberger, appeared and beat all the Germans in the dressage championships at Aachen. She repeated this success the following year, took the 1975 European title and the 1976 individual Olympic title. Switzerland, however, can only claim part of these glories for she usually rides German horses and trains outside the country, in Austria. However, there are others appearing in the lower echelons of international competition and they were able to give Christine Stückelberger enough support to earn for the Swiss team the bronze medal at the 1975 European championships, and the silver medal at the 1976 Olympic Games. Switzerland has restored her position amongst the top dressage nations.

In eventing, the results have neither been so spectacularly high, or low. The best results were at the Rome Olympics when Switzerland won silver and bronze medals and, although out of the medals, were well placed in 1972 at Munich. They usually achieve places at international events, but the premier awards have eluded them.

Driving is the sport of which the Swiss can be justly proud of their competitors They were some of the earliest participants in the first international combined driving championships of the 1960s, and have carried off World and European championships.

The future for Swiss equestrianism looks promising as equestrian activities at the national level are booming. In a nation of
6,000,000 people, there are 45,000 horses and 25,000 riders. Of
these riders, 3,500 have licences for competitive riding and since
1966 this figure has been increasing at a rate of $10\frac{1}{2}$% per year.

THE HORSE

One of the major problems for this increasing number of riders
has been horsepower. Their country did not produce home-bred
Swiss warmbloods. The Swiss successes have been gained on
French, German, English, Irish, Polish and Swedish mounts.
These have been brought into the country mainly by dealers who
are a feature of Swiss equestrian life.

There are a number of prosperous large-scale dealers with
yards of one hundred, or more, horses, ranging from Dublin
champion hunters to cheap, and rather second-rate, riding horses.
The small colourful dealer found in England and Ireland has
little chance to compete against the big Swiss set-ups. These latter
have arisen because of the need for a large capital outlay to cover
transportation costs and to gain the benefits of importing in
bulk. Also the government controls importation through the
issue of licences and the 'big boys' monopolise the supply of these.

The expense and limitations of depending on this source of
horse power has been realised and steps are being taken to
develop a Swiss warmblood. Previously, the lack of home breeding
was blamed by many on the nature of the country. It was said
Switzerland was not suitable for rearing horses, but history does
not support these arguments.

Horses must have been indigenous to the country, for one of
the earliest references to the horse was found in Switzerland at
Schaffhausen. It was an engraving of a wild horse which was
drawn around 1,000,000 B.C. Then, in 1064 Switzerland established
one of the earliest studs. The monks of the Cloister Einsiedeln
started systematic breeding, developing a breed known today
as the Einsiedler, a stocky horse suitable for riding, transportation
and driving. Large numbers were exported up to the middle of the
nineteenth century, and Napoleon must have been one of the most
prolific purchasers. He bought 30,000 Swiss horses for his armies.

With the development of the railways, the horse's functions in Switzerland became limited to transportation in the mountains and agriculture. This placed the demand on a heavier draught animal and the Jura type became popular. Towards the end of the last century the government stepped in to encourage breeding. Their major development was to set up the national stud on the outskirts of the old Roman capital of Switzerland, at Avenche.

Today, Avenche is still the national stud, but breeding is no longer confined to that of the heavy horses. Mechanisation of farms meant fewer of the Jura type were needed, but the government found the demand for other types of horses was growing. They realised a good Swiss warmblood could reduce the country's import bill and raise the status of Switzerland as an equestrian nation.

The person who has done much of the campaigning for this redirection of national stud policy is its director, Dr. Hector Lewenberger. A rotund Swiss German, Dr. Lewenberger bubbles with enthusiasm about his task to establish a new Swiss breed. He has good qualifications, for he is a veterinary surgeon by profession. Previously, he was head surgeon at the cavalry depot in Berne and, as such, was a member of the commission that travelled Europe to buy hundreds of horses for the Swiss army. This helped to develop both his ability to recognise a good horse and to establish contacts for future purchasing.

Dr. Lewenberger has taken on the enviable challenge of developing a breed, with the financial backing of the government. He has chosen three basic features to aim for: character, movement and performance. To achieve these he has purchased stallions from Sweden, Germany, England and France, to form a nucleus of 80 warmblood stallions and 3 thoroughbreds. These have not ousted the old Swiss breed entirely, as there are still 40 stallions of the Jura type producing horses for the army and the occasional farmer.

All the national stud stallions are based at Avenche, where 375 acres of fields surround the stud buildings and run down towards Lake Mortan. A further 250 acres, 1,000 metres up in the Jura mountains, also belong to the Ministry of Agriculture and the youngstock graze there in the summer.

About 60 mares are kept at Avenche, which are representative of some of the best lines of French and Swedish blood. However, Dr. Lewenberger is aware that at present the stud is top heavy with stallions and is using, generally, a too low standard of mare. This he is aiming to correct, firstly by further purchasing and secondly by following the stud book for stallions started in 1973, with one for mares.

As in most other European countries the stallions have to prove their performance abilities. They are subjected to tests which are some of the stiffest in Europe. At 3 years of age they go through the same dressage, jumping, cross-country, driving and racing tests used in Sweden. Two years later, at $5\frac{1}{2}$ years, there are even more rigorous tests. Expert horsemen in each field try the stallions in their particular discipline. In show jumping, the expert is usually Paul Weier and he will ride the horse over a small course. Once tested in the three equestrian disciplines, conformation is assessed, fertility considered and produce examined. Successful candidates can only then, deservedly, look forward to many years' service at the national stud.

During the breeding season many of the stallions from Avenche are sent to regional station depots. There are 67 of these scattered throughout Switzerland, so that breeders have few travelling problems.

Breeding is the main activity at the national stud but, as at Flyinge in Sweden, there are also annual sales for mares and geldings. In addition, like Austria and some of the state studs of Germany, the horses and facilities have lent themselves to further uses. The stallions themselves partake in equestrian sports; most notably driving. Robert Doudin drove a team of Swiss bred stallions into second place, behind his compatriot Dubey, in the 1973 European championsips at Windsor. This success had a sequel which illustrates the following the stud has acquired, for when Doudin returned to Avenche the citizens lined the streets to welcome and cheer the success of the members of 'their' stud.

The cross-country course on the stud is used to test instructors and young riders as well as the stallions. Also in co-operation with the Club Abbye Rouge, the stud has built further fences to create one of the few permanent cross-country courses in Switzerland. Situated amongst the fields bordering Lake Mortan, this is

SWITZERLAND

used for training and for one of the major horse trials of the year.

The stud followed the example of the Swedes and now runs courses for young people who wish to learn about stallion work and how to look after them. This has the great public relations benefit of involving outsiders as well as giving equestrian education to young people.

The Swiss may have been tardy in developing a Swiss warm-blood, but the way they are tackling the subject today indicates that before long their breed may well be on a par with the proven Swedish and German warmbloods.

RIDING CLUBS AND CENTRES

The Swiss riders should look forward to a better future now that their government is financing the development of a home bred warmblood. However, the Swiss government's contribution to equestrian activities is limited to breeding. Every other aspect of Swiss riding is in private hands. Even the riding club, which is the backbone of Swiss riding, is dependent on private finance. There appears no lack of private funds, however, as the country has a few rich bankers around!

Every rider belongs to one or more of these clubs and generally relies upon them to house his horse, or horses. However, the clubs have an even more important role in Switzerland than elsewhere in Europe, for it is through them that all horse activities are organised. Draghunting, which is common in Switzerland, is run by clubs throughout the country. Each horse trial is run by a club as is every horse show. Even the Geneva show, their premier official international show, is run by clubs.

Many clubs offer secondary entertainments, such as a bar, a coffee room, and members spend time in each other's company, both on and off horseback. These clubs vary in standard, type and purpose rather more than in other countries as there has been no powerful central organisation, or local government laying down standards, as in Germany and Sweden. The clubs have sprung up in response to individual initiative. Some only having a social and administrative role, organising functions such as hunting and competitions. The more influential, however, are those with indoor schools and stabling run on commerical lines.

Typical of the latter is the Manege de Grange Falquet at Geneva. The instructors there spend most of their time teaching beginners to ride. Smart Genevois, children of foreign diplomats and the ordinary Swiss come here, to go round and round in circles, often without stirrups and with a voice booming at them to keep the heels down, heads up and the like. Instruction standards are good and with a few years of exercises, no stirrups and continuous circles the students develop seats of which most Britains would be envious.

Outdoor work is limited because of the weather and the hostility of farmers towards riders crossing their land. The result is that a Swiss rider's upbringing is mainly spent in an indoor school. They learn much more about the theory of riding, about the right aids and the best position from which to apply them. This contrasts markedly with the more natural British education – riding across country, learning to cope with the unforeseeable and to react quickly under different circumstances.

The Grange Falquet Club at Geneva is a thriving concern, with a ramshackle collection of buildings housing coffee rooms, offices, stalls for nearly 100 horses (most of whom are owned by the school), and two small tatty indoor arenas, where class after class is given instruction from 7 in the morning until 10 at night. Outside, surrounded by the houses of Geneva, there is a small sandy area containing permanent and coloured obstacles. There is an air of scruffiness surrounding the club and there is no prospect of improvement, for that sandy paddock and the sheds containing indoor arenas and stalls are due to be demolished and replaced by modern offices. Plans exist for a modern luxurious development of the club in the country. But the Grange Falquet has many members. They like it as it is, and so far private finance for a modernised establishment has not been forthcoming.

Perhaps it is the misfortune of the premier equestrian centre that has made them cautious. This showpiece of the nation is in the small village of Murton which lies between Berne and Lausanne. Over £1 million has been spent to provide the club with every possible facility. The top Dutch trainer, Anthony Paalman was engaged to school pupils, later his role was taken over by Paul Weber. However, despite these first-class trainers and facilities offered, the modern stables are nearly all empty, and

the enormous indoor school, with such luxuries as water sprink-
lers, is little used. The Swiss seem to prefer the less elaborate
facilities of their existing clubs and perhaps also the situation of
Murton is too remote and the fees too high.

The EMPFA

Switzerland's most famous riding centre is the Eidgenössicsche
Militär Pferde – Anstalt (EMPFA), the federal military horse
institution in Berne. The school was built about 1890 and was
one of the last European cavalry schools to be established.
It earned a high reputation for dressage. Officers came from all
over the world to learn the Swiss formula which was based on
the best points from the German and French schools. The Swiss
had acquired their knowledge in a similar way to the Swedes,
sending their officers to courses at the best schools in Europe.
The officers returning from these sorties to France, Germany
and Italy, however, did not have the same magnificent and extensive outdoor facilities that the Swedes created at Strömsholm.
At Berne there were only four acres of undulating paddock which
were crammed with natural obstacles, and an outdoor dressage
arena. Most of the training had to be done in the five indoor
arenas. Switzerland was then, as it is now, indoor orientated, and
dressage was a natural specialisation.

The residents at the Berne cavalry school won medals in
international dressage arenas (1950s and 1960s) when competitors
in military uniforms were becoming rare. The continuation of
the Swiss cavalry after the last war was justified both because of
its unusual organisation and the nature of the Swiss terrain
which made men on horseback a viable means of defence.

The organisation of the Swiss army is rather different from
that of other countries as it is made up for a large part by part
timers. Every Swiss youth is conscripted into the army for a period
of basic training. Then he is posted to the reserve for a number
of years, during which time he is required to return for a brush
up session each year.

Those who chose the cavalry spent four months being trained
at the headquarters. When they returned to civilian life they took
with them a horse of their choosing, for which they paid the
government half its cost. In return for this bargain purchase,

they and their horse had to partake in cavalry activities for three weeks each year.

About 800 horses were distributed to these part time cavalry members each year. The system meant that the cavalry obtained inexpensive man and horse power; Switzerland had more educated riders and more horses for competitions. Everyone seemed to benefit and it was no wonder that this form of cavalry survived so long.

With every male Swiss having to go into the army, and with every equestrian minded one choosing the cavalry, Berne and its artillery counterpart at Thoune, were the major influences on Swiss riding. Their principles were passed on to the young Swiss and acted as a uniting factor in this diverse country. The cavalry also provided an exceptional opportunity for talented young men to make riding their career. A small nucleus of professionals were employed as civil servants by EMPFA and which included in the 1950s and 1960s both the Olympic medal winners, Henri Chammartin and Gustav Fischer.

Since the mid-1960s the system has been doomed. Government ministers are on record as promising to put an end to this 'out of date' service. In the age of atom bombs even this more economical and useful cavalry organisation has come under fire from the modernists.

Fervent campaigns of protest have as yet saved the Swiss cavalry from the same fate as those in Britain, Sweden, Denmark and Germany. Its end, however, although delayed, seems inevitable. The thin dignified commandant of EMPFA, Major Pierre Eric Jacquereod wears an expression of sad resignation for during his ten years of office he has known there was no future to work for. He has known that a cloud was hanging over one of the last pillars of the old way of life. Sadly he, like so many of the officers of a disbanded cavalry, feels unable to adjust to train civilians.

In its heyday the Berne depot housed over 1,000 horses and provided anyone stationed there with an outstanding opportunity to learn and succeed in equestrian activities. They could ride numerous horses each day including trained schoolmasters on which they could get a 'feel' of how jumping and dressage movements should be done. The horses too had a good chance of producing their best ability. Their training was done under the surveillance of an expert; and as there were so many horses there was little pressure to bring them on too quickly. It makes the path for today's private one or two horse owners look torturous in comparison.

One of the unique features of the Swiss Cavalry School was that the horses were drawn from countries all over the world. Only since the 1970s has the Swiss warmblood been used in any numbers, and in the heyday of the cavalry it was the Irish, French, Polish and Swedish warmbloods that filled the stables. A small group of Swiss buyers travelled over Europe to buy 3-year-old horses. They purchased hundreds of inexpensive horses each year, and from this number, one or two could be relied upon to become high grade competition horses. The best were housed in exclusive stable blocks, and there was one for each discipline. This division according to the horses' speciality proved that particular warmbloods have their metier. The dressage block was normally full of Swedish horses, the jumping and eventing stable of Irish and French. It was only the driving block which had a cross section of nationalities.

Today many of the hundreds of stables are empty. The few remaining members of the cavalry dressed in their grey, sombre, workmanlike, uniform appear to carry a burden on their shoulders. They can remember the days when the cavalry was responsible for all the famous Swiss riders: Fischer, Chammartin, Klaxell, Mosel, Weier, Mohr and Blixenstoff. Then Berne was the mecca of Swiss riding, now, not only the principles but the facilities too, seem doomed, for of the numerous plans put forward to save the depot, none as yet has met with the approval of all the affected parties.

THE TRAINERS

In this individualistic country, the trainers have been unusually independent. There has been much less control over the type and standard of instruction than in other European countries. However, the Swiss have become aware of the possible drawbacks of this, and are working towards a greater uniformity. An association has been formed, L'Association Suisse de Profession-nels de l'Equitation et Proprietaires de Maneges. The man behind its formation has been Paul Weier. He has led the campaign to provide a set of guidelines and principles which will form the basis of every Swiss instructor's teaching.

These guidelines have been achieved at meetings of the association which have been held twice a year. A topic (for example, 'The Young Horse') is discussed, and agreement reached as to how the matter should be approached. The principles adopted bear the influence of those present, the works of W. Museler and the manual of the Swiss cavalry. The decisions are then documented and all instructors in Switzerland encouraged to teach within this framework. But this aim of uniformity has aroused controversy. Some think it suppresses individual flair and impedes the rise of new ideas; but in Switzerland where so much individualism has been known to hinder progress, it may prove an effective solution.

The association hopes to implement this uniform doctrine through the education of young instructors. Switzerland is one of the last countries to provide a system for equestrian education and to call for qualifications. Until the late 1960s anyone who could prove experience of teaching could apply for recognition as a professional instructor. Now two grades of instructors have been established. Three years as an apprentice at a selected school, followed by an examination, qualify the student for the first level. Two further years working as an instructor, followed by a week of examinations and successful candidates earn the title of maitre d'equitation.

The attempt to promote equestrian uniformity in this diverse nation is a fascinating adventure. If the Swiss succeed, no longer will a child be told to grip with his knees at one school and to hold them open at another. No longer will the Swiss Germans be encouraged to jump with the precision and collection of the Germans and the Swiss Romands with the speed and loose rein of the French. The aim now is to agree which are the best points to follow and to teach a consistent method – a 'Swiss Style of Riding'.

The need for more good Swiss trainers is great. It seemed likely that retired cavalry officers would fulfil the demand, but few have been able, or wanted, to make a successful transition from the training of disciplined recruits to that of independent civilians.

Henri Chammartin

Henri Chammartin, the 1964 individual Olympic gold medallist and a world champion of dressage, is of the right age to pass on his knowledge to a new generation. He has done so but appears to find the horses more responsive and understanding pupils than riders. He trains by riding the horse, obtaining the results and then perching his trainee on top. His difficulty is expressing clearly how it should be done, for his riding came naturally and without any need for thought and analysis. Consequently Henri Chammartin will continue to be a great aid to many riders, but may not achieve the same success as a trainer as he did as a rider.

Roland de Weck

Chammartin's great partner in the days of glory, Gustav Fischer, helps a number of the young riders, but one who reaped fewer competitive successes is now becoming a respected ex cavalry trainer. His name is Major Roland de Weck, an ex master of equitation at Berne. His present fame is derived from knowing the 'tricks of the trade', rather than as a relayer of Berne's principles. His greatest lessons are in the art of showmanship and learning how to produce the best effect for the judges. For example he says most tend to ride an oval circle, which is avoided by aiming to complete a larger circle. De Weck is an astute gentleman, and his ideas have been beautifully reproduced in a book called *Messiers à vos Cheveaux*. It, like his training, has a different approach from the mere relation of equestrian information. Each dressage movement is discussed, the difficulties involved listed and corrections suggested. These corrections are made by way of exercises (French fashion). It is then much easier for the rider to put right the fault than by just being told what the mistake is.

Georg Wahl

Despite all his good ideas, de Weck cannot claim majority support in Switzerland. Paradoxically the one nearest to this is a foreigner. He is the Austrian Georg Wahl (see Austrian section). After leaving the Spanish Riding School he set up at a town riding school near to Berne. Here he acquired a very special pupil –

Fraulein Christine Stückelberger. She showed enough talent to compensate for any lack of interest by the others and, as her parents were wealthy enough to buy good horses, it did not take long to turn her into the most exciting new dressage star of the 1970s. When Georg Wahl moved back to Austria to train at Rietverein Wiesenhof, just outside Salzburg, Fraulein Stückelberger's horses went with him. After this departure an increasing number of other Swiss realised that he was a great loss. He has been persuaded to return for clinics and the National Federation is mustering support to make him national trainer.

Paul Weier

Paul Weier, ironically, despite his escalating influence on training methods and style, manages to keep equestrian sport a mere hobby. This dark haired, balding Swiss German is by profession a hotelier. At the equestrian centre of Elgg, north-east of Zurich, he runs his own hotel.

Paul Weier, who is still only in his forties, has become the focal point for most of the new developments in Swiss equestrian life. He has risen to this position on the back of one success after another. In the 1950s he was the Swiss dressage champion three times. In the 1960s he was the national three-day event champion three times and in his metier, show jumping, he has six national championships to his credit. It is a remarkable feat of horsemanship to achieve such a variety of successes in a country where each of these disciplines is highly competitive.

Paul Weier's ability was developed early, as his mother, a Swiss dressage champion, could give him instruction. His brother Louis channelled his equestrian interests into that remunerative Swiss occupation of horse dealing. He set up his stables at the family's equestrian centre at Elgg, providing a constant supply of equine material. Then Paul Weier went to the source of the best possible instruction of that time – the cavalry. He rose to the rank of captain before reverting to civilian status and taking over his hotel.

The Weier family's establishment has now become an unofficial national equestrian centre. Instructors and show jumpers queue up to stay in Weier's hotel. The American show jumpers with their consistent riding are Paul Weier's heroes and he has become a Swiss amateur version of the great coach, Bertalan de Nemethy. He has helped to form a team of riders who are beginning to put the name of Switzerland to the forefront of the show jumping nations.

The first principle Paul Weier advocates is for the rider to establish a good position, even over the fence. Not like his, he quickly adds, for despite his strong ideals he has ungainly habits such as legs going back over the fence.

Students at Elgg spend much time jumping fences without stirrups aiming to establish a jumping position in which they look between the horse's ears with a straight back and with a direct line from the point of their shoulder through their hands and the reins to the mouth of the horse. In this position the rider finds it easier to carry out his purpose which is to regulate the horse's speed, length of stride, collection and rhythm in respect to the fence they are about to jump and the one that follows it.

With a young horse the rider's interference should be minimised as in early jumping the green horse should learn to look after himself. With experience, the role of decision maker is reversed, the rider becomes increasingly influential, until the ultimate – the Olympic standard – when he should make 90% or more of the decisions.

Paul Weier's training is hard, as he places great stress on discipline. His horses receive a high standard of dressage schooling and many hours in draw reins to lower their heads and supple their backs, but he allows more freedom when developing the horse's ability to jump.

Weier is also a protagonist of gymnastic exercises over low fences. The lines of parallels and uprights, basic to Bertalan de Nemethy's schooling and that of his fellow trainer in America Jack le Goff, are found in many corners of the Elgg equestrian centre.

In jumping, as in dressage, the style emerging in Switzerland is a combination of ideas from other countries. The value placed on dressage, the constant demand for obedience on the flat, and, at later stages, over the fences, stem from German ideas. The importance attached to a good seat, gymnastic exercises and the encouragement given to young horses to look after themselves, is more typical of the French and American approach.

Jean Franco de Rham

One of Paul Weier's most valuable supporters is Jean Franco de Rham, the Swiss Romand who trains most of the top Swiss French jumpers. The internationals Francis Racine, Carol Maus and Peter Reid are amongst his pupils and being taught according to Weier principles, means they can go off to international training courses at Elgg without any fear of confusion.

Jean Franco de Rham has an imposing appearance with a tall burly figure, a shock of black hair and a neat drooping moustache. He looks as if he could earn money as a film star but his first career was much less glamorous, he was a television and radio technician. He only trained riders during his spare time until the early 1960s when he was offered the post of chief instructor at the Manège de Génève.

He threw security to the winds, and ventured into a professional life with horses. For one year he worked from 6 in the morning until 10 at night, taking classes which were, predominantly, at novice level. He claims it was a wonderful background, as with so many hours teaching he learnt quickly how to put ideas across.

Then the opportunity arose to set up on his own at the Manège La Gambade which is on the outskirts of Geneva. There he has a luxurious wood lined indoor school and an enormous sand outdoor school filled with both permanent and moveable obstacles. He bought horses, trained them, used them as schoolmasters and found he sold them very quickly to his pupils. Now his stables are full of jumpers, and eventers; some originally bought by him but all now belonging to his, predominantly affluent, pupils. This type of training set-up, without school horses, with no facilities for taking classes and only catering for boarding and training the privately owned competition horse, is unusual in club orientated Switzerland.

Basically, de Rham follows Weier's guidelines, but he would not be Swiss if he accepted them in their entirety and failed to use a few variations. His French nature makes him unsympathetic towards excessive discipline of the horse and, consequently, moderations creep in. He is suspicious, too, of uniform style for riders. French instinct for freedom and individualism does not take too willingly to such restrictions. De Rham likes to train within the style of the horse and rider. For him the character must not be suppressed by regimenting or imposing particular methods upon them. He illustrated this theory with the example of the young international Swiss rider Peter Reid, who gained high honours when jumping in the most ungainly fashion. Now, retrained, his style is good, but his successes have been fewer.

De Rham has reservations, too, about another aspect of the discipline demanded by Weier methods. He regards the draw rein as a valuable aid to achieve a good head position and obedience in the shortest possible time, but he feels it is a dangerous gadget. Only high class riders are capable of using it with benefit and even in their hands persistent use can suppress the horse's character. The Germans might want machines as their jumpers, but de Rham does not.

De Rham has accepted Weier's basic aims, but has applied them less strictly and with a more flexible approach. He has a good basis for comparison, as his earlier master was Nelson Pessoa, one of the 'greats' in the show jumping world. This brilliant competitor from Brazil used Geneva as his base in the early 1960s, when he did as much for French Swiss jumping as Weier is now doing for the whole of Switzerland.

Until Pessoa's arrival, the Swiss Romands naturally practised the French approach – push, push, faster, faster – and generally on a loose rein. The only problem was that they did not have such good horses, or riders, as their neighbours. The result was pretty dangerous and Pessoa's success made them sit up. They started to copy his steadier approach to fences, his demand for obedience on the flat and his use of gymnastic exercises over small obstacles. De Rham, after hours of watching and discussing these methods with the maestro Pessoa, adopted them whole-heartedly. They proved to be a stepping stone towards Weier's principles.

Jean Franco de Rham's greatest personal success has been in dressage. He has twice been the best Swiss professional champion in this discipline and yet he only has a small number of pupils. He claims the failure to appoint a national trainer and an inconsistent policy towards the sport has led to a feeling of disillusionment with dressage in Switzerland.

De Rham claims that nearly every rider he has taught suffers the same basic faults. The most serious of these is a poor seat and he encourages his pupils to get into the habit of removing their stirrups for the first few minutes of their riding day. Another fault is that they nearly all ride from their hands and de Rham stresses that it is the legs that should control, as the movement comes from behind. Then there is normally a tendency not to realise the importance of the outside rein for most apply the inside rein too strongly and disturb the equilibrium.

An interesting aspect of de Rham's training is his reluctance to ride his pupils' horses. He thinks that the pupil should feel for himself what is going wrong and not get the horse to carry him. He only leaps on if the pupil claims his demands are impossible, then he needs to prove his point!

Training juniors

The type of training for junior show jumpers in Switzerland is impressive and comprehensive. There are regular courses at regional and national level. At these, dressage and caveletti work is covered in addition to leaping high fences. The Swiss are conscious of the danger of riders taking short cuts and want to develop at an early age knowledge of basic groundwork. They are also aware of the importance of suppling exercises for the rider as well as the horse. Consequently, the potential jumping stars are encouraged to take up gymnastics, and swimming.

Ernst Lance

Relatively few of the Swiss riders go eventing and considering this the Swiss have been exceptionally successful. Credit for this, at present, is largely due to the national trainer, Ernst Lance who is a former international rider. His base is at Rheinfelden, near Basle, where there is one of the most extensive ranges of cross-country fences in Switzerland. Potential international riders come to him two or three times a year, and he also travels around the country to give individual lessons.

Once again a compromise style has emerged. Ernst Lance favours the long rein horizontal style of the French in dressage and the more collected and precise approach of the Germans when jumping.

ADMINISTRATION AND COMPETITION

With the cavalry disbanded, the Swiss riders will become increasingly dependent upon the National Federation for directing policy. As one would expect in Switzerland, it is a very democratic organisation. Clubs and societies are the members of the Federation and they send delegates to a general assembly. This directs policy, but is too cumbersome to decide much. The real power is in the hands of groups of experts. One group has been formed for each of the four disciplines – jumping, dressage, eventing and driving – to be responsible for regulations and policy and to oversee the riding clubs' organisation of competitions.

The FN organises courses for judges and course designers as well as for riders. In jumping, the FN has overcome the problem of finding universal support for a single trainer by naming three for adult jumpers and five for the juniors. The best riders are then given options as to whose course they wish to attend.

In the competitive sphere, the FN provides no financial support. It does, however, control the riders, for as in France the FN issues licences to compete. These are only awarded to those people over 12 years of age who have successfully completed a dressage and jumping test. It is a system which encourages all riders to have a basic knowledge of horsemanship.

The riders receive small rewards in most competitions. There is little sponsorship and, as in the Scandinavian countries, successful competitors are given silver cups, rather than money, to pay the bills. With money not playing an important part, the grading system is based on points gained from victories. A sensible aspect of this grading is that horses are allowed to compete in any grade below them on a handicap basis. In eventing they receive penalty points and in show jumping a few higher fences are included in their course. It is a simple way of helping to restore a horse, or a rider's, confidence and not forcing either beyond their capabilities.

Show jumping

The opportunities for riders to compete are more abundant in show jumping than the other disciplines. Top level show jumping, despite the lack of high financial rewards, has the same neo-professional atmosphere of Germany, France and Britain. This has arisen because of the prestige value of the sport. The Swiss consider it rather smart to own horses and although some owners ride their own horses, the standard of the advanced grade jumping is too high for most of the part-time amateurs. The majority of good horses are ridden by talented professional type riders and owned by either the rich, or the dealers, who use competitions to show off their wares.

Of the riders dependent upon rich owners, Francis Racine is one of the most successful. Monsieur Maus has put at his disposal some 11 or 12 horses which are stabled in Jean Franco de Rham's yard. However, riding these is only a hobby, for Racine is employed as chauffeur to Monsieur Maus.

Paul Weier rides for a wide range of owners, as well as producing horses for his brother Louis the horse dealer. Paul Weier's petite, pretty, wife Monica has no difficulty in obtaining mounts in her own right. She is one of the world's leading lady riders. As Monica Bachman she took the Swiss national championship for 1966 and 1970. She also put up very creditable performances in the Olympic Games of 1968 and 1972.

Most of the other leading riders come from horse dealing families. There is Max Hauri who has the exceptional record of riding in both the show jumping and three-day event teams at the Munich Olympics. His father has a stable renowned for high class and expensive horses.

Then there is Marcus Fuchs the brilliant young rider who, when still a junior, wrested the 1973 Swiss championship from his elders. This entitled him to be one of Switzerland's two representatives in the World championships at Hickstead in 1974. His father is a natural 'wheeler dealer', with an abundant supply of reasonably priced horses and usually a few cows too! Fuchs senior started in this trade by bicycling to Czechoslovakia where he found the horses were within his meagre price bracket. Now his bicycle has been replaced with a Jaguar car (highly prized in Switzerland), and his stable contains a 100 or more horses. He has been helped to achieve success and prosperity by rearing an exceptional family of riders. His children are proving to be some of the most promising riders that Switzerland has ever produced. The eldest, Marcus, is already a star and a junior champion of Europe, but Thomas and Heidi are also proving their talent, and dominate the classes for their age group.

Eventing

Contrasting sharply with show jumping, is eventing where the amateur approach flourishes for there is little public interest and, therefore, minimal prestige value is attached to this sport. Few events are held, the clubs that do the organising find that eventing is much more complicated, expensive and time consuming than the arena activities. Also Swiss spectators have not yet discovered the entertainment value of eventing and there are rarely more than families and friends pacing around the cross-country course. This means the clubs usually lose money so there are only two or three one-day events, and about four three-day events in the entire season.

The Swiss riders have, however, quite a number of combined competitions – jumping and dressage, or cross-country and dressage. This helps the riders to gain competitive experience and their international results have been very creditable.

Tony Buhler, a pig farmer, has been representing Switzerland at Olympic and Continental championships for many years and his successes include the Olympic individual bronze medal in Rome. Then there is Paul Hurlimann who was one of the best placed individuals at Munich in 1972. Both these successful riders help in the administration of and training for, eventing. Paul Hurlimann has a young pupil who promises to give the English and Germans some strong competition. His name is Beat Bohli. At 15 he won the 1972 Swiss open championship, and not satisfied with this, in the following year he was first and second in the championship. Even these successes are not the product of a professional approach for he is a student who relies on his family's help. His father, who runs a business in Zurich producing beer and minerals, is his head groom.

Dressage

The mid-1960s marked the end of military leadership and domination of dressage and for a few years there was much confusion amongst the civilians who took over. No consistent approach to dressage could be decided upon as the opinions of judges varied as to what they were looking for in a trained horse and the dressage tests were altered frequently.

Improvements, however, are likely. An expansion of judges' conferences and courses to decide upon guidelines is helping to reduce the inconsistencies. Also, in 1974, a new set of fourteen tests were brought into operation which were all devised by the same people at the same time. The principles upon which they were created are worth examining.

The basic aim was to make a logical progression from the simpler movements out of which the more demanding could be developed. The movements used and the way which they should be performed were based on Berne's conventions. Practical considerations were also borne in mind, such as a lack of perfect judges meant that each movement had to be easy to mark, that the rider as well as the horse should be tested and that spectators were vital for the development of the sport and they had to be entertained by eye-catching movements.

Driving

Driving is a rapidly developing sport. It started with the cavalry who drove all their remounts during the early stages of training, Henri Chammartin even drove his advanced dressage horses. Consequently, when in the early 1960s international driving classes began, Switzerland was able to send out representatives from the Berne depot. They won at the Aachen show in Germany and, in 1973, the Swiss team brought home the European title. A. Dubey was their star and he captured many honours including the 1972 individual World championship and the 1973 individual European title. Domestic interest was aroused in this sport at which the Swiss shone and classes were held in increasing numbers all over the country. The 1974 World championships were staged in Switzerland at Frauenfeld, but Britain was able to win the team title, relegating the home team to second place.

Circus

The final equestrian activity for which Switzerland is renowned is its circus. Freddie Knie of the Swiss National Circus is one of the world's greatest exponents of equestrian acts. In England, high school circus acts earn little respect from horsemen and are a feature of fewer and fewer circuses. On the Continent, however, it is another matter. Horse acts are of a high standard, the talents of circus riders recognised and their methods examined by the equestrians. They are renowned for producing a spectacular performance in a remarkably short time and it is Freddie Knie who is probably the best of them all. He does use gadgetry and the horses can be allowed to specialise in the movements which come easiest to them, rather than being tested for all round ability as in Grand Prix dressage. Nevertheless the skills involved are enormous and dressage riders can learn a great deal from Freddie Knie. Indicative of this is the fact that one of the world's most successful trainers, Georg Wahl, spent time with Freddie Knie.

Despite the critics' claim that the overall standard and interest in Swiss dressage has declined, the country still has her stars. Freddie Knie delights audiences all over Europe and the petite, blonde, Christine Stückelberger on her great Holstein Granat has challenged her elders and the stronger sex. She has beaten all comers and electrified spectators with dressage performances that have brought a burst of excitement to the sport. She and Granat can combine cadence, fluency and spontaneous impulsion with precision and accuracy. She has been able, as have her country's greatest riders before her, to adopt methods, principles and styles which suit her and are derived from both the French and the Germans.

CHAPTER FIVE

DENMARK

THE Danes and the British enjoy a special affinity, perhaps stemming from the conquest of Britain by the Vikings of Denmark 1,000 years ago. The Danish way of life, their food and pastimes are not unlike those in Britain. Their approach to the horse, their style of riding, the type of horse they like, is also in sympathy with that of the British. However, a more socialist background has led to different priorities.

In this socialist country incomes are rarely very high or low, and everybody has to work to earn them. Those who choose to make their careers with horses have a hard existence. Grooms look after 12 or more horses, trainers ride up to 14 horses a day. For the majority of riders, however, riding is their hobby carried on in the early mornings, evenings and weekends.

The feature of Danish equestrian life is the predominance of truly amateur competitors who rarely have the time or the money to own more than one horse; but who are schooled by professional trainers in luxurious riding schools. These part time riders have no hope of challenging the top ranking show jumpers from the neo-professional nations, nor have they much prospect of shining in the time consuming sport of international eventing; but they have excelled in dressage for in this discipline trainers and good riding facilities are more important than riding many horses, or having extensive competitive experience.

The first Dane to earn glories for the country was a lady. Liz Hartel became the first woman to win an Olympic equestrian medal, when in 1952 she took the individual dressage silver medal. To show it was no fluke, she won the same medal four years later in Stockholm.

These successes inspired her compatriots, and dressage became 'the' glamour sport. Young people concentrated their attention on producing piaff and passage, rather than jumping high fences. The result is that the Danes are now one of the most successful nations at dressage, although only a tiny percentage of the population is horse orientated. They have the smallest horse population of any of the equestrian minded nations, 40,000, compared with France's 519,000 in 1973. Yet the Danes were fourth in the dressage at the Munich Games of 1972 and their representatives are always well placed in the European and World championships.

THE HORSE

Denmark has a long tradition of horse breeding. In the flat open country of Jutland, the farmers have bred islander ponies and large war horses called Juts for centuries. As in neighbouring Germany and Sweden it was the royal family who gave their leadership to the development of the nation's horse. Between 1562 and 1862 the most famous of the Danish royal studs flourished north of Copenhagen at Fredericksborg. Repeated imports of horses of Andalusian and Italian Neapolitan blood were made. These were the most popular breeds of the time, used to lighten and give class to the heavier work and army horses. It proved to be a good combination with the indigenous small, thick set, Danish horse, and a new breed was produced. It was called the Fredericksborg after its birthplace. They were sturdy, showy, horses that became popular all over Europe as parade and school horses. They in their turn were used to improve the French and even the Lipizzaner breeds.

Then, in the last century, the demand for the Fredericksborg began to fall. Other countries were producing their own breeds. Also Denmark grew more socialist and the royal studs were disbanded. Some farmers continued spasmodic and uncontrolled breeding in Jutland, but most of Denmark's best riding horses were of foreign origin.

In recent years the Danes have realised the benefits of having their own source of equine power and their potential as an export earner. A central breeding administration (The Danish Sportshorse Breeding Association) has been set up. It has no government backing, there is no national stud, but private individuals

have laid down standards, provided encouragement and assistance to breeders. German, English, Polish and Swedish blood
has been imported to be used as basic breeding stock.

Approved stallions now have to pass a series of tests for conformation, fertility and ridden performance. This was started in
the early 1960s and already the Danish Sportshorse has earned
itself a good reputation. Germans and Dutch are crossing into
Jutland and whisking away horses that are cheaper than those in
their own countries.

RIDING CLUBS AND CENTRES

The nature of the country and way of life has made the riding
club basic to the Danish rider's life. Most of the population is
concentrated around Copenhagen, where riding outdoors entails
wending between houses and along roads with heavy traffic
roaring by. Clubs with indoor schools, outdoor jumping arenas
and cross-country fences were more attractive places to ride at
and more and more were formed as the riding population grew.

The hard-working Dane wanted someone to take over the
responsibility of looking after their one horse. The social-
minded Dane wanted somewhere to enjoy their pursuits and
where like-minded horse enthusiasts could have fun in their free
time. The riding club with facilities for exercising the horse, and
entertaining the rider, suited the Danes better than keeping the
odd horse in a backyard.

The first major club, the Sportsrideskolen, was set up on the
outskirts of Copenhagen before the First World War. It was a
very 'smart' venture where the rich from Copenhagen kept their
horses and practised the art of dressage. Today it is still a focal
point of equestrian activities but together with the rest of Denmark
has been 'socialised'. Members are amateurs who rarely own more
than one of the 110 horses stabled there and the school is busiest
in out-of-work hours, before 8 a.m. and after 5 p.m.

The Sportsrideskolen has traditionally been the most important
riding centre, but it can no longer boast of the best facilities. In
1970 a few miles north of Copenhagen, a luxurious equestrian
establishment was opened. It consists of a massive building containing 120 stables, a full sized dressage arena, lungeing and warm-

ing up arenas, a cafeteria and comfortable spectator galleries. It is called the Holte Riding Club. It cost about 5 million Danish Kroner, and provides a centre which the Danes can be proud of. Shows are a popular feature, and up to 400 people start in the dressage competitions held on many winter Sundays, when immaculately dressed competitors riding braided, gleaming, horses perform tests all day long. They can be watched from the glassed in members bar. For the young Danes this is a great way to spend a winter Sunday, riding, drinking, eating, talking, watching and all in the warm. In the summer they transfer to the outdoor arenas, which also contain permanent obstacles for the jumping classes.

In between shows the club still hums with activity. For many of the 1,000 members, the Holte Club takes up most of their spare time. It stables their horses, and they can ride them there, in between watching and talking. Depending on their standard and inclinations, they can choose their trainer. Instructors are available to help them and to ride their horses. The aim of the club is to provide two trainers from the top league for dressage and show jumping, and one younger person to instruct in basic work.

Holte may be the showpiece of the Danish equestrian world, but there are many other clubs which provide riders with similar, if not quite so elaborate opportunities. In Jutland another 60 × 20 metre indoor arena has been completed and all over Denmark there are clubs with indoor arenas lined with stables, outdoor jumping rings and coffee bars. These facilities which make serious concentrated riding easier, also help equestrian enthusiasts get together to discuss, learn, criticise and generate enthusiasm, which enables these part-time riders to become surprisingly successful.

THE TRAINERS

The trainers are one of the Danes' greatest assets. In recent years the country has developed a system which is producing a relatively large number of talented young men in this occupation.

There are three levels of professionals in Denmark, trainee, riding master and horse master. The first three years are spent as a trainee. On completion of this period and with examinations passed, they become riding masters. In this capacity they can remain at Danish schools, but most try to take the 'long course' at the magnificent Swedish school of Strömsholm. After three years as riding master they can take the examinations which, if passed, qualify them as horse masters. Many of the young Danes who earn this title spend further time abroad to extend their knowledge. This thorough and extensive apprenticeship is practised by young men of high calibre, who, when they finally take up a position, can command high fees. A successful horse master can look forward to a remunerative, if demanding, life.

Enken Hansen

One young man who is enjoying such success is Enken Hansen. Born at the end of the Second World War, he was one of the last horse masters trained in the Danish cavalry. When he set up on his own he experienced a few lean years. But today the old barn, which was his only indoor school, and the few ramshackled stables have been added to. A private sponsor has built for him an indoor school 50 × 20 metres, a large number of new stables, an outdoor arena filled with permanent obstacles and a sand ring. An abundance of pupils use these excellent facilities, most being under 30 which tends to produce a friendly and informal atmosphere.

Enken Hansen himself has the air of self confidence which often emanates from one who has succeeded through his own initiative. His style of riding and training suggests this too, being definite and demanding. His greatest successes have been in the show jumping field and he is responsible for the training of a Danish show jumping champion, Briget Holt Hansen. It is typical of the Danish way that this lady, one of the most successful show jumpers, is a scientist by profession and arrives at 5 a.m. to train. This lack of opportunity for more full time pre-occupation with sport makes the trainer indispensable.

Gunnar Andersen

The Danes' greatest trainer, Gunnar Andersen, took this indispensable role of the trainer to its ultimate limit, by enabling genuine amateur riders to reach Olympic medal winning standard.

Gunnar Andersen does this by approaching his training with a long-term view and few commerical considerations. He establishes a tri-partite relationship: a horse, a rider and himself. He sets about understanding and becoming friends with both his human and equine pupil. He rides the horse a great deal finding out its weaknesses and teaching it more than most riders, certainly much more than part-time ones, are capable of doing. The rider he attends to in an equally thorough fashion, but there is no instant transformation, no quick answers. He knows what he wants and gradually he moulds them into his ways. The final result is that both can ride the horse, both have schooled, with remarkable competitive success.

Inevitably, such a development is a long term project, but it is one in which Andersen has his heart. The pupils on the week long courses that he takes in America and England usually come for instant transformation and improvement. They may provide him with more remuneration, and a refreshing change, but he is not a 'rapid results' commercial trainer. To fully use his great talents he needs pupils with time, patience and dedication. The Danes are very fortunate that this great trainer prefers to enjoy his life back in his homeland, rather than to earn vast sums of money trying to teach the world how to press the buttons that make a horse perform.

He looks typically Scandinavian, tall, thin with a wrinkled healthy face. He enjoys making fun of himself, his pupils and friends and cannot contain occasional bursts of boyish giggles. His eyes twinkle at humorous moments, and they have been used to take in a great deal during his life. He is one of the few dressage stars who has never had formal training, for his equestrian education was gained through watching and experimenting.

His education started early for his father was a Corporal Major in the Royal Hussars and as most of the best Danish riders came from this regiment, there were great opportunities for watching. His father encouraged him to try it out on horseback, but many would have found it an off-putting method. Andersen was given horses to ride, but no stirrups. For seven years he had to rely on balance to remain in the saddle and the result is one of the best seats in Europe.

Gunnar Andersen's only formal training came when major

Danish influences (including the King's) were used to enable him
to go to the Swedish cavalry school. The brilliant young rider
after much lobbying was accepted as the first civilian pupil at
Strömsholm. For one and a half months he trained with the
riders from the most successful equestrian country in Europe.
He rode across country without reins and stirrups and practised
dressage on the school horses. Sadly this unique opportunity
and stimulating life was ended with the invasion of Poland by
Germany. Gunnar Andersen returned to the hard slog of trying
to earn a living out of horses. He became the instructor at the
most important Danish riding school – Sportsrideskolen. For
twenty-eight years he worked there and at one time he rode up to
15 horses a day.

For the last ten years he has had less arduous duties. After a
two-year sojourn in America, he returned, in 1965, to work at
Mrs. Enid Ingemann's school north of Copenhagen, but after
a few years moved to Barthus, before becoming the private
trainer to Mr. and Mrs. Jensen. When I was in Denmark he was
based at Barthus, a riding centre with a vast indoor school which
was, as Gunnar Andersen pointed out, warm even in winter.
This made him very happy for he said, with another twinkle in
his eyes, that he is getting 'so old'. By normal trainers' standards
he might be considered so, he was born in 1909, but he does not
look it as he jumps on to a horse, pipe still in his mouth and,
after a few discreet pushes and pulls he produces a transformed
horse.

When I was with him, his day started at 7 a.m. with Aksel
Mikkelsen, who runs a chain of men's clothes shops, coming for
a lesson before work. Mikkelsen rides an ex-show jumper –
Talisman – a white horse flecked with black and which is a
thoroughbred/Hanoverian cross. They have been dressage
champions of Denmark on three occasions. Gunnar Andersen
worked Talisman for 20 minutes, then Mikkelsen took over.
Andersen stood on the side, pipe still in his mouth and in a quiet
voice issued the odd commands and correction, but the three of
them knew each other so well that there was very little that needed
saying.

At 8 o'clock another of Andersen's small band of pupils came
out. There were others, however, that stabled their horses at the

school, and received their advice from one of a number of instructors at Barthus. Occasionally they had the benefit of the odd comment from the maestro, but to enjoy a regular hour's individual instruction was the right of a very few. The pretty Annette Tegedal was one of them. She was the Danes' great hope for future Olympics. Her horse Charlie Brown who proved too slow on the racetrack has an overwhelming number of assets for dressage. One could see how much Andersen enjoyed educating him, and his delicate young lady rider. Her chic attire, and Danish good looks made an elegant picture on the thoroughbred.

Charlotte Ingemann is another decorative rider. Also a successful one, she represented Denmark at the 1972 Olympics on a failed racehorse – Souliman. After the Olympics a lack of funds persuaded her to sell Souliman and to find a young replacement. She took on an enormous but exciting gamble. She came to England and bought at Newmarket, a stallion rejected for stud work because he had savaged two of his grooms. Hardly one's notion of a dressage horse, but he was very handsome. Charlotte Ingemann had him gelded, spent months handling him personally and hacking him around the countryside. Eventually he was ready for Gunnar Andersen to start work. The horse had to be a success, she could not afford another, but Gunnar Andersen is fascinated by this type of challenge. Under training which is neither as domineering as the Germans nor as erratic as the French, it is possible that this horse will find a niche in life, which he enjoys and will be able to shine at.

So Gunnar Andersen's morning passed. On each hour until 12, another horse and rider appear. They were of varying standards, but all five partnerships had been chosen because they were thought to have the potential to benefit from the help of this dedicated and talented man.

The afternoons were more light hearted. Gunnar Andersen visited clubs, took group lessons and taught show jumping. He enjoys this discipline although he knew the Danish were unlikely to be very good at it. Show jumpers must ride their horses all the time and have many of them. This is difficult in Denmark, where riders have to work to earn the money to pay trainers and to keep their horses. Today Gunnar Andersen has a chance to work against the odds, as he now trains in a private show jumping yard. With this great trainer behind them, perhaps we might see some Danish international show jumping stars in the future.

Gunnar Andersen is a great believer in variety and the stimulus this brings to training. All his dressage horses go for enlivening hacks across country. He encourages people to go jumping. For him, riding, like life, must be fun and not a narrow, single minded search for success.

His riders have to combine fun with very hard work. The early winter months were spent without stirrups. Andersen always sets an example by riding without them himself, and even goes to gymnastic classes to keep his back and shoulders supple. He wants his pupils to ride with a deep, firm, upright seat; yet at the same time to be relaxed. He is aware this can take courage. Fit Grand Prix horses are powerful and sensitive creatures; they can easily dislodge nervous riders.

The horse he looks for as a dressage star should move well, have a light and easy stride, and be calm without being lazy. Thoroughbreds are his favourites but he is aware that for many of them collected movements are difficult. It is when they start to do piaff and passage that the shortcomings of this breed are exposed. He has been disappointed on many occasions with thoroughbreds which have worked well until this advanced level and then failed. Now he starts to develop the passage after about a year, in order to test the horse's capabilities. He has learnt to avoid wasting time on horses that cannot make it.

This early experimenting with advanced movements does not mean that the basics are sacrificed. Andersen believes it is essential to start with the ABC of riding – a good seat for the rider and a horse which goes forward using his hocks, walks, trots and canters correctly and is on the bit.

After establishing the foundations Gunnar Andersen starts to teach his horses one of the key points of his methods, the half halt. A stronger pressure on the reins is accompanied by leg and/ or seat aids. It is used as a means of making the horse listen, place his hind legs under him, and to make the neck and mouth more supple. At more advanced stages the rider uses it as a warning that a demand for a movement is imminent. For Gunnar Andersen this simultaneous push and pull is basic to dressage riding. His horses are continually subjected to it and his riders are asked to apply it to correct head positions, to achieve more collection and suppleness and as a precedent to any movement.

This use of the half halt is a feature of Andersen's dressage riders. He claims that all high level riders apply it whether they call it something else, or are oblivious to the fact. But the French at Saumur would question him. They say that if a horse is in equilibrium there is no need to apply this form of correction. They claim to be positively against its use as it can inhibit their – 'god' – impulsion.

Another feature of Andersen's training methods is the variety of movements used. Horses are rarely allowed to work for more than one hour in the school, but during this time they are subjected to a wide variety of demanding exercises. As soon as the ABC of training has been established, then the horse is taught leg yielding, shoulder in, rein back, turns on the forehand and counter canter. These are then used continuously to keep the horse alert, and to make him supple.

It is the flying change for which his pupils (horses and riders) are particularly noted. He does not start to teach his horses this movement until they respond correctly to his key point, the half halt. Then he goes into a highly collected canter; almost coming back to the halt before applying the aids, and if necessary the outide leg is reinforced by the use of a long dressage whip. If there are any problems he often uses the half pass at the canter from which to develop the change.

The passage and piaff he develops when riding. With his great ability there is rarely any need for long reins or whips to achieve the greater collection and the longer suspension required in these Grand Prix movements.

Gunnar Andersen's method of training is to teach the horse, which can then give the rider the correct feel, rather than to tell the rider how to do it. I never heard him shout, and in fact he rarely said much. Probably pupils hardly know what is happening to them.

Andersen pointed out to me one young man who had been working for days on his own in the school. Andersen had passed only the odd remark to him, but told me that this rider was likely to have a different style in a few months. He was a young professional trainer, who had returned from an apprenticeship under

PLATE 18
Gunnar Andersen.

PLATE 19
The Danish dressage champions, Aksel Mikkelsen and Talisman closely watched by Gunnar Andersen.

Bubi Gunther, the leading German trainer. He was riding in a typical German manner working the horse for a short time only, but very, very, hard. He was using continuous extremes, canter to halt and vice verse, rein backs and the like. It was a harsher method of achieving the same result as the half halt. The rider's style as well as his methods were different. His back was very straight and rigid in comparison to Andersen's pupils. He also inclined behind the vertical. Andersen felt he could not achieve so much in this position for when not upright the use of the aids through the seat bones was restricted.

Although this German style did not look so elegant, or delicate, as that of Andersen's pupils one had to remember that it was the fashionable and the most successful method of our times. The horses ridden in this manner are usually warmbloods. They are more powerful and less sensitive than the thoroughbred, also impulsion has to be supplied rather than coming naturally. But Gunnar Andersen prefers the thoroughbred which requires a more sensitive approach. Perhaps it is the different types of horse which appropriate these different styles and methods. The world, however, tends to follow the Germans; probably wisely. The warmblood's temperament means that tact is not a premium, mistakes can be made. A thoroughbred leaves less room for error. Few other than Gunnar Andersen have both the ability and the sensitivity to elicit the performance of which the thoroughbred is capable.

Liz Hartel

Gunnar Andersen's most successful pupil – Liz Hartel – now trains, but, not other competitors. Instead, on a good will basis, she helps professional trainers and handicapped children. She has a particularly sympathetic interest in the latter for she has achieved her success despite partial paralysis.

Liz Hartel was born into a horse minded family. Her mother was able to train both her and her sister to become Danish dressage champions. This was not the result of a specialised equine education. Liz Hartel used to steeplechase, three-day event and show jump; but finally decided her preference was for dressage. For her the pleasures were so much greater, 'It is like music and dancing every day. Jumping is only fun over the fences, the rest of the time one has to ride a stiff unsupple horse.' Her great satisfaction is to get the horse to work the way she wants it to. She went further, for she uses dressage not merely to improve the performance of the horse, but the conformation as well. She looked proudly at her rather heavy Oldenburg horse. When she bought him, she claimed that his only attractive feature was his head. However, by using the right exercises, she had built up those muscles which have turned him into a handsome horse. It seemed that this mastery over the way a horse went and looked, was her great pleasure.

It is extraordinary that this spirited lady can master her horses. It can no longer be by strength, for after becoming Danish dressage champion she was struck by polio. It left devastating after effects for a rider. She could not move her legs, nor her left arm fully. However, she had that one characteristic essential to success – determination. She had another too in her trainer Gunnar Andersen. That tri-partite relationship was established between the elegant mare Jubilee, the able but handicapped rider Liz Hartel, and the great trainer Gunnar Andersen. The result was the first Olympic medal for a lady rider.

Her visit to the Horse of the Year Show following her success at the 1952 Olympics was a memorable occasion. It aroused great interest in dressage in England as her display enraptured the British public. The whole performance was against the odds. Mares had rarely been successful dressage horses, but here was Jubilee ridden by a pretty but handicapped woman carrying out the most difficult movements with lightness and elegance. The show too had a special sparkle which emanated from her vital and spontaneous personality. She used to change the figures according to her moods. The conductor of the accompanying music had a demanding job that week, but the delight of the crowd, and the deafening applause, must have been full compensation for the extra work.

With the passing of Jubilee, Liz Hartel has not found another comparable partner. Her recent history has been full of disasters. One horse after another has become ill or lame. Despondent, she no longer trains thoroughbreds, but has chosen heavier, tougher, horses. Today this fragile lady can be seen riding enormous and powerful horses at the Holte Riding School. With the help of the German trained instructor, Dubceck, she is managing to produce precise, elegant movements out of these hefty beasts.

For her, collection is the most important aim and she believes a great deal of driving in long reins makes it easier for the horses to achieve the advanced collected work when she rides them. She says the piaff and passage may come relatively easily in the riding school; the difficulty really starts when it has to be produced, not just when everything is right to do so, but on a particular spot, at a precise point, in the test.

It is to be hoped that this great personality will have better fortune with her horses in the future, and will be able to offer a challenge again in the dressage arena. She will, however, have to face formidable opposition from a youthful set of riders. The Danish dressage arenas are full of determined young men and women.

ADMINISTRATION AND COMPETITION

The organisation which controls and encourages equestrianism in Denmark is the Dansk Ride Forbund. It has the unique task of protecting the amateur spirit, of retaining the approach to riding which makes it fun and not merely a professional work. The organisation has not called upon any government help to make this possible, nor does the money to run the organisation come from sponsors intent on publicity. Its only source is from members and some, like Mrs. Ingemann (at whose school Gunnar Andersen trained), have left large bequests.

The cost of running the organisation is not high as there is no complex network of controls. Most riding clubs are members which run their own shows and group together to run district shows. It is only the open shows which are organised by the Ride Forbund, and there are only five such shows in the spring and five in the autumn. At these shows prize money is rare, the most that is normally offered is a token to buy equipment in saddlery shops. The Danes ride for the love of it, not for the money. It is only at international shows in Denmark that prize money is given, as they have to attract the more mercenary foreigners!

The Copenhagen international show is held spasmodically in

a park on the outskirts of the capital. Among the international riders it is one of the most popular CCIO's. The courses are built by Kragh Andersen who makes them inviting and original and incorporates the banks, ditches and walls found in the permanent arena. To add to the attractive venue is the sporting amateur atmosphere that the Danes exude. To them taking part in show jumping is fun, as well as winning. It is a refreshing approach for the riders from nations where this type of sportsmanship is all too often part of history.

The zenith of international competitions for the Danes came in 1974 when they staged the World dressage championships in the grounds of Christianborg Castle. Sadly the home team was one of their weakest for years. They had been hit by misfortunes. One of Gunnar Andersen's pupils, however, proved to be an admirable exponent of his fluent and sympathetic style. This was Mrs. Ulla Peterson, with her 1972 and 1976 Olympic mount Chigwell.

It was unfortunate that another of Andersen's young pupils, Sven Larsen, was prevented from representing Denmark through lameness of his horse. It would have been appropriate for him to have enjoyed the honour, for his family are largely responsible for Danish equestrian administration and success. His father is president of the Ride Forbund; his mother, Grete Larsen, has been Danish dressage champion; his sister, Ann, has represented Denmark in the junior European show jumping championships. Like most young men Sven thought his riding interests lay in jumping fences. But when a Swedish horse by Jovial, kept hitting obstacles, he thought he would try some dressage with him. Sven enjoyed it, became successful and joined the Danish team. Now he would not consider reverting to jumping.

This is the feature of Danish riding. The number of riders in their teens and twenties who are enthralled not by leaping into the air, but by performing exacting movements. Bitten Soderberg, a university student and Grand Prix rider, said 'It is the thrill of moving a muscle and getting the required reaction from a horse'. These enthusiastic young riders have brought honour to their country. They have turned dressage into a glamorous sport which has stimulated great spectator interest.

Show jumping and eventing are overshadowed disciplines in

Denmark. These sports are truly amateur, and although the riders can have fun at the frequent shows held at home they rarely venture on to the international circuit. In the days of the cavalry, eventing was taken more seriously. At the cavalry head-quarters of Noestved, it was part of the officers' curriculum to take part in competitions and eventing was the popular sport. In fact the Danes were in the lead for an Olympic team gold medal at the 1948 Games when a technical elimination in the final show jumping phase robbed them of this great glory. Today as in other countries the Danish cavalry has been run down. Now there are only parade horses and officers do not compete. The amateur civilians have neither the time nor the money for this demanding sport at the international level. As for show jumping, the Danes go eventing to have fun rather than as a means of success.

The other bit of fun that the Danes enjoy is draghunting. Followers don their pink tail coats and top hats to chase riders carrying fox brushes. The line is prepared and the fences are not too high. But on All Saints' Day, in common with most European countries, they hold celebrations for the patron saint of horses – St. Hubertus. The draghunt plays a great part by having a line which is longer and has higher fences than on any other day of the year. Also the number of followers is multiplied, so ensuring appropriate celebrations for the saint who watches over the source of so much of their fun – the horse.

The horse in Denmark is to be envied. He is usually the sole property of a doting owner, has comfortable facilities in which to be worked and a knowledgeable overseer to ensure he is ridden to the best possible advantage.

CHAPTER SIX

AUSTRIA

AUSTRIA is renowned for equestrian activities. The performances of the Spanish Riding School are probably the best known equestrian spectacle in the world. For many millions, Vienna is connected first and foremost with white stallions. Its role as an international conference and music centre is of secondary fame.

It is the riding skill of a mere eight to twelve horsemen, the members of the Spanish Riding School, that has created this fame. In the past riding in Austria was an exclusive activity, restricted to only a small number of people, primarily, as in France, the rich upper classes. It was not until the 1960s that ordinary folk found that riding was possible and within their means. This tardy democratisation of riding is due largely to the unsettling disruptions Austria has suffered.

The First World War brought about the break up of the Hapsburg Empire and thirty years later came more disasters. Peace after the Second World War brought with it a loss of wealth, a change of boundaries and, for ten years, occupation by the English, American, Russian and French armies. Planning, organisation and the impetus needed to get things going were difficult under these conditions. Nor was there much of a spirit of patriotism to help, for the Empire had been a federation of states, not a country. The Austrians of today are a collection of races, ranging from the Slavs in the South, to the Germans in the North. There is no bond of nationalism between these peoples.

The horses are equally varied as practically every breed is represented and used in Austria. With this varied collection of races of humans and of horses, no typical Austrian style, or approach to riding, has emerged. In fact many of the recent influx of riders have not been taught at all, but simply set off into the countryside. Hacking across their beautiful land they have learnt by trial and error how to stay on and control the animals.

With this healthy, amateurish approach towards riding, it is not surprising that the Austrians have had their most consistent international successes in the European rural championships. As we discussed in the chapter on Sweden, this championship is one of the few genuine amateur international equestrian contests.

There is a wind of change, however. The international show jumper Hugo Simon was born with a dual German/Austrian nationality. After a German education he chose to become Austrian and riding for Austria, he has become one of the world's most successful show jumpers. In 1974 he was equal third in the men's World championship at Hickstead and two years before, fourth in the individual event at the Munich Olympics. This has excited and encouraged his countrymen. The results are already showing. The Austrian juniors startled the establishment by winning the junior European show jumping team championship of 1974.

In dressage the Austrians have not yet won major classes but their competitors at international shows put on better and better performances with each year that passes. Hans Max, Hans Mraz, Ines Badewitz, Robert Schifter are amongst those building an improving reputation for their country.

In eventing, too, the Austrians began to make headway in international competitions. In the 1973 European championships at Kiev their representatives, F. Croy and W. Rihs finished 11th and 13th as individuals. At the 1974 international event at Colombier they took many of the honours, but since then major prizes have eluded them.

THE HORSE

The most famous Austrian horse, the Lipizzaner, is not suitable for the budding young Austrian competitors. Consequently, the Lipizzaner only makes up a very small percentage of the total equestrian population, about 300 out of nearly 60,000 Austrian horses.

Nor is the Lipizzaner a truly Austrian horse. The foundation stock was imported from Spain, hence the name the Spanish Riding School.

The Lipizzaner was bred by the Moors, who crossed the Berber, Arab and Vilanos horses from the Pyrenees. The produce earned a reputation for being an exceptionally intelligent and gymnastic animal and Archduke Charles, intent on making the High School at his court the equal of any in Europe, imported in 1580 9 stallions and 24 mares. He established a stud for these prized beasts on the bare stony land of the hamlet of Lipizza in Karst (now part of north-west Yugoslavia). It was bleak country but had been proven by both the Romans and the Venetians to be a top-class breeding ground.

The experiment was successful. The Lipizzaner became the Vienna court's most popular horse and more were imported from Spain. For 350 years they were bred successfully at Lipizza, but on several occasions their safety has been in jeopardy. French wars at the end of the eighteenth and the beginning of the nineteenth century necessitated four evacuations. Then the First World War brought more permanent disruptions. In 1915 the stud was evacuated to Vienna and the peace settlement took Lipizza into Italian territory.

The Austrians had to find a new stud and they chose an old military one at Piber, a village in the South. Some 143 acres of rugged land was available to rear their Lipizzaners and the seventeenth-century Piber castle was used as offices, adding a distinguished tone to the establishment.

The Second World War brought further evacuations. During 1941 and 1942 the Lipizzaners were collected from Yugoslavia and Piber and taken to Hostau in the Bohemian Forest. When in 1945 the allies advanced into the area the German stud officials made sure all the Lipizzaners fell into the hands of the American army, who quickly evacuated them westwards to avoid conflicts with the approaching Russians. The Lipizzaners were saved and after a spell at the stud of St. Martin, returned to their home at Piber.

Today there are between 130 and 150 Lipizzaners at Piber which have been bred according to strict principles. Foreign blood has been introduced to improve the strain. During the eighteenth century Italian, German and Danish horses were imported and cross bred. Again in the nineteenth century Franz Joseph imported Arabs from Syria and Palestine. Now the

Austrians are satisfied with their product, new blood is rarely introduced and moderately close inbreeding occurs. The guiding principle, at all times, is performance ability. Only those stallions who have proved to be outstanding workers at the Spanish School are ever used. The only problem is that the best performers are disputed for by both the school and the stud.

The mares, too, are chosen for their performance ability. They are broken both to the saddle and to harness, tested and, if weaknesses are revealed, they are sold without being bred from.

The product of this careful mating of proven performers is a horse between 15 hands and 16 hands. The Lipizzaner is born dark and does not turn grey until about the age of 7. The odd bay is never used for breeding, but the School at Vienna always has one in training, as it is considered good luck. The most well known assets of these Lipizzaners are their intelligent temperament, their gymnastic ability and their great life span. They are very slow to mature, but then can often work for 20 or more years, and many of them reach the age of 30.

The stallions spend their working life in Vienna where their daily routine is a half hour session of hard training six days a week. This extreme domestication of the Lipizzaner is partially offset, however, during the first 3 years of life which are spent on the wild rugged lands at Piber. Here the horses learn to develop their natural instincts and are free to establish their own character. The Lipizzaner has a life of contrasts.

The Lipizzaner may be the most famous Austrian horse, but many other types are bred. The most popular Austrian horse is the Haflinger. These tough palomino coloured ponies were traditionally bred in the Tyrolean mountains. Their great assets are endurance and sure footedness. They have been, and still are, a major form of transport in this mountainous country. They also provide the many pony trekking tourists with an excellent means of viewing Austria.

The national stud for warmbloods is at Stadt Paura, which lies between Linz and Salzburg in the north of Austria. It has been used as a stallion depot for nearly three hundred years and now contains a wide variety of stallions. Some have an Austrian birthright, but there are, too, imports which come mainly from Germany in the shape of Trakehners and Hanoverians. The

Austrians, like the Swiss, are buying proven breeds of warm-bloods, so they can breed for themselves a high-class riding horse.

RIDING CLUBS AND CENTRES

The Austrian riding club, although central to the rider's life, is more similar to the British versions than those in the rest of Europe. Of the 200 Austrian clubs, the majority have no indoor school or elaborate facilities. They have been formed solely with the intention of collecting together like minded equestrians in order to promote social and competitive activities. As in England there is no vast government finance and the few boasting of high-class facilities are privately supported.

A common activity of these clubs is a cross-country ride (hunting is banned). Like the Danes, Austrian riders celebrate All Saints' Day and the patron saint of horses, St. Hubertus, on horseback. I enjoyed one such cross-country event. We set off walking and trotting lackadaisically across the rolling hills of southern Austria and along tracks through pine forests, stopping frequently to converse and drink schnapps. Then in the final moments the club split into the goers and non-goers. The former galloped headlong over a few fields and jumped the occasional ditch, the remainder took a shorter route home, which meant they could remain in the walk.

The day's riding was rounded off with a dinner that evening. The club members, including countesses, dentists and butchers tucked in to suckling pig, more schnapps, and more discussions about horses. These Austrians loved riding and horses, but for fun, and as a means of viewing their lovely country. Most had never been trained, and had never been inside an indoor school. Instructors, at least good ones, have been rare in Austria.

TRAINERS

Anyone in Austria can become a riding teacher and the National Federation has only recently started issuing certificates for those officially qualified. The FN, however, has become more aware of the dearth of good instructors and they are taking steps to give the growing numbers of Austrian riders the chance to learn by serious instruction as well as by riding across country.

In 1972 the FN started instructors courses at the national
stud of Stadt Paura. Excellent training arenas and permanent
obstacles already exist as they have long been in use for the
training of warmblood stallions. The aim is to make Stadt Paura
the Warendorf (Deutsche Reitschule) of Austria. Courses are
now held for beginners, grooms and potential instructors.
Activities include dressage, jumping, cross-country and driving.
It seems that Austria is quickly getting her riding on to a more
professional basis.

Hugo Simon

At present the ambitious Austrian rider has a limited choice
of trainers. For the show jumpers, Hugo Simon is the most popular.
He runs courses for Austria's most promising riders at the luxurious Austrian riding club at Linz, close to the German border.
He, like Hans Günter Winkler, is a top ranking international
show jumper, so that he can pass on to pupils his personal
knowledge of high level competing. It does mean, however, that
he must remain unremunerated for the training otherwise he
must relinquish his amateur status and a place at the Olympic
Games.

Georg Wahl

For eventing, the Austrians occasionally go across the border
to one of the best trainers in the world – Pohlmann. In dressage
the Austrians have a world class trainer of their own in Georg
Wahl, who was a member of the Spanish Riding School. He was
promoted to the position of chief rider in 1967. However, he
found the pull of competitive riding strong, and competing is
not thought consistent with Spanish School principles. He
therefore decided to resign and since 1971 has concentrated on
training competitors and competing. After a brief spell in
Switzerland, he returned to the Wiesenhorf Club which is just
outside Salzburg. There he trains privately owned horses and
riders who come with their own mounts. His teaching is based
on the classical principles of the Spanish Riding School, but
adapted to the demands of today's competitions.

Wahl is the Austrian national dressage trainer, taking the best of his countrymen in both pure dressage and the dressage side of eventing. So far, as mentioned in the chapter on Switzerland, his most famous pupil is Fraulein Stückelberger, who spends much of her time at Wiesenhof.

With their unrivalled education of the Spanish Riding School it is surprising that there are not more former members helping the Austrians. The reason has been that the attractions abroad have been greater, both in terms of facilities and finance. The benefits of their training at this classical school have been scattered internationally, rather than remaining in the homeland. England is fortunate in having one of the best of the ex-chief riders.

Franz Rochawansky

England is Franz Rochawansky's second home since leaving the Spanish Riding School. For eighteen years he lived in Holland where the opportunities and the remuneration were attractive enough to take him from Austria. His benefactor was the director of the Daf automobile empire, Mr. Vandoorne. His important pupils were Vandoorne's two daughters and they were able to work in a school which was one of the most lavish in Europe. Every provision for training, even video tapes, was available.

England is now his base, although he takes off on trips to give clinics to the riders all over the world clamouring to learn from him. He says he likes the English because of their natural horsemanship. A background of hunting and jumping means that they are not frightened to sit on a horse that bucks and they have a natural 'feel' for the horse.

The pupils who know him well call him 'Rocky' and these include nearly all the British star riders. Everyone respects this talented enthusiast. Great bushy eyebrows practically cover up narrow slanting eyes which gaze piercingly at the horse and rider he is training. He makes constant remarks in broken English and totally involves himself in improving each combination, whatever their standard. He will do this both by telling the rider what to do and by getting on himself to make the horse perform. One of Rochawansky's great assets is that he is able to tackle a problem both by perceiving and by feeling. Most trainers specialise either in riding the horse or instructing the rider. Rochawansky is one of the few who is capable of shining at both.

Franz Rochawansky's principles, like Georg Wahl's, are those of the Spanish Riding School adapted to the demands of competitive riding. No one can question the basic authority of this extraordinary school.

THE SPANISH RIDING SCHOOL

Revered equally by both the layman and the expert, the Spanish Riding School of Vienna is, for the serious rider, the ultimate place for training. For the spectator, it is the most famous and sought after equestrian display.

This reputation has developed because, whilst other schools have been created and destroyed; whilst styles and methods of riding have been argued over, experimented with and varied; the Spanish Riding School has continued to function using the same standards and methods. For 400 years it has taught riders and has passed on to them the art of classical riding by word of mouth. It has become a guardian of history and the guardian of classical riding.

The first mention of the Spanish School was made in 1572. The 'vogue' for High School was just beginning in the courts of Europe. Frederico Grisone of Italy had written his book *Eli Ordini di Cavalcare* establishing a more thoughtful approach to riding. The French abounded with ideas about the art of riding, but it was popular for more than aesthetic reasons, as the training of horses in leaps, kicks, lateral movements and general obedience, saved lives when fighting on horseback.

The members of the Hapsburg dynasty which ruled Austria were as fervent equestrians as were any other royal family. They imported Spanish horses and so began the famous School. Although the schools of Florence, Versailles and Hanover earned equally great reputations they broke up due to political turmoil. The Spanish School survived the European wars, the disintegration of the Hapsburg Empire and the occupation by Germans, Russians, American, French and English.

The School's home too, although not built until 150 years after the formation of the School itself, still survives. Emperor Charles VI was responsible for the building of the Winter Riding School, one of the last and most magnificent pieces of baroque architecture in Vienna. This high, predominantly white, hall is lit by three vast chandeliers and is a stunning memorial to the splendours of the Hapsburg Empire. An era when only the nobility could watch the performances, but today every type of spectator from countries all over the world fills the two layers of galleries. They come to watch the white stallions in the same displays that were performed when Vienna was one of the most influential cities in the world.

There are public performances two or three times a week. Then, every one of the 1,100 seats is filled, most of them having been booked weeks in advance. To the strains of Riedinger's Festlicher Einritt, 8 young stallions, who have only completed one or two years' work, enter the hall. The riders in their brown dress coats, white deer skin breeches and black elongated top boots, doff their bicorne hats to the portrait of the founder – Charles VI.

The performance is a polished exhibition, dramatically presented, but for those who want to understand the methods and approaches of the school, the training sessions are more revealing. 60 horses have to be exercised six days a week. Between the hours of 10 and 12 on non-performance days spectators can watch how the riders prepare their stallions.

Grooms lead into this historic arena, 6 to 8 Lipizzaner stallions for each session. The horses look tiny, a mere 15 hands to 16 hands, but they are so deep that even a tall man does not look out of proportion on their backs. The portrait of Charles VI is still saluted and the work begins.

During the half-hour session each combination carries out their own individual schedule. Most start with a relaxing rising trot, but the odd one will go straight into a non-demanding piaff. Nearly all begin their lateral work at the walk. In some of the half-hour sessions one of the stallions is worked with long reins, from the ground. During every session there is a top rider on the sidelines passing the odd critical remark and words of advice to those riding.

I was struck by the severity of the riders' demands, but the Lipizzaner is one of the most intelligent breeds of horses and those familiar with them say they need strong corrections. In comparison with Germany the variations in pace are not so extreme and the extensions not so extravagant.

The riders' speciality is their collected work. They have chosen the horse which has the temperament and gymnastic ability necessary to obtain this. Thoroughbreds could not be ridden in the same way, but with the Lipizzaner the passage, the piaff and the schools above the ground (the leaps into the air which are a form of release from collection), would be the envy of any rider.

Competitive success is not one of the aims of the members of the Spanish School. There is a feeling there, as at Von Neindorff's in Germany, that classical principles should not be skated over in the haste to achieve competitive success. The Spanish School is there to preserve these pure methods of riding. Their horses, too, are not suitable for the demands of competitions. The Lipizzaners shine in the collected movements, but they are too small, do not have great power to extend and cannot cope with the variety of movements asked for in competitions.

The tasks of a member of this unique riding school are clearly defined and exclude competitive work. Instead they must act as the custodians of the classical equestrian principles and demonstrate them to the public. They must influence the general standard of riding by taking pupils and they must promote the Lipizzaner breed of horse.

The responsibility of carrying out these aims is borne by about twelve members of the Spanish School. They are divided into full riders, assistants and apprentices. They are all employees of the Austrian Ministry of Agriculture and, as such, subject to its controls. However, the director of the Spanish School is a very powerful man and derives great prestige from the position. It is he who formulates the policy and so decides how the Spanish School's great influence should be directed in the equestrian world.

Colonel Podhajsky

The director who kept the school going through the turmoils of the last war was Colonel Podhajsky. The members and the horses of the school were hurried from one base to another to avoid bombs and capture. The school survived and Podhajsky made the post-war period a busy one. He was aware of the need to justify the existence of the Spanish Riding School in a time when many traditional institutions were being disbanded. He organised trips around the world to build up its international reputation. The school has to date, performed to admiring audiences in Germany, Holland, Belgium, England, Italy, Denmark, France, Spain, Portugal, America and Canada. Also in the early 1950s foreign students were taken to promote a more universal acceptance of the principles of the Spanish School. From England, Charles Harris, Robert and Yook Hall were some who benefited from this move.

Hans Handler

In 1965, after twenty-five years of outstanding work, Colonel Podhajsky retired. Hans Handler, a former member of the Spanish School, a Colonel in the Austrian army and renowned as a judge and lecturer, took over the directorship. Sadly his term of office was shorter than Podhajsky's for he died whilst riding his horse in the autumn of 1974. With no obvious successor after his startling death, the control was divided. Colonel Albrecht now runs the administrative side and Herr Lauscha, the chief rider, the equestrian aspects.

The Spanish Riding School is traditionally a school for riders, for it is through its pupils that it hopes to cultivate classical riding in its purest form. The danger to this policy is excessive commercialisation, turning the school into little more than a tourist attraction.

The problem is that the government expects the school to earn a good income to support its existence. The Austrians are not so generous as the French, who heavily subsidise the Cadre Noir at Saumur. This means more performances are needed at the Spanish School to provide the money, and less time is available to train riders.

In recent years very few students have trained at the School, other than young Austrian citizens. The latter are usually accepted when in their mid-teens and need have little riding knowledge. They are taken as apprentices and learn to look after horses as well as how to ride them. Most of these apprentices stay for ten or more years, graduating to become an assistant rider, but then the problems arise for the school. As soon as these young men become competent trainers, they are tempted by offers of high salaries and good facilities elsewhere. However, what the Spanish

PLATE 20
Annette Tegedal riding Charlie Brown, with Gunnar Andersen instructing.

PLATE 21 (*above*).
A training session
at the Spanish
Riding School.

PLATE 22 (*right*)
Work from the
ground during a
training session.
The pillars used
for piaff and the
airs above the
ground can be seen
in the foreground.

School loses, the world gains from this spread of invaluable knowledge.

The school does accept students from abroad, but only if they can prove exceptional ability. They come to Vienna from all over the world to take a series of rigorous tests. When they have passed this test, it does not guarantee their acceptance. A number are now waiting to be told that the Spanish School has time to teach them. Only two from England, John Lassetter and Daniel Pevsner, have been told this in the last decade and both passed their tests more than two years before they were allowed to join the school.

Thus, it is largely upon the young Austrian students that the school relies to preserve its role as a trainer of riders. They are taught according to the principles practised for hundreds of years. However, each recent director has been a strong personality and as such exerts a different emphasis on the basic methods.

Colonel Handler had an aesthetic approach. For him a dressage rider was an artist and the horse his medium. Together they were able to produce a work of art. The horse and rider could become a single creative personality.

In achieving this, Handler emphasised the importance of mental communication. To elicit the most from a horse, a constructive inner relationship had to be built up between horse and rider. Harmony between man and animal is the end result and it takes pure hard work, as well as talent, to achieve it.

The rider must first learn to sit correctly so that he can keep his balance on the horse. Then he must learn to 'feel', to be able to know what the horse is doing, and is about to do. Handler compared it to training the ear in music. Finally the rider must become familiar with all the aids, but the subtle use of these is only possible after he has learnt to 'sit' and to 'feel'. At the Spanish School this is largely achieved by work on the lunge.

The seat advocated at the Spanish School is an erect one with the hips slightly forward, the weight on the seat bones and the knee closed on the saddle. This differs from the French who push their seat bones forward so that they tend to ride behind the vertical, and they also like an open knee. The seat at the Spanish School is more like that of the Germans. Although many of the Germans have developed the idea so far as to be on the verge of riding with a hollow back.

At the same time as developing the correct seat of the pupil, the trainer will encourage his subject to express what he feels is happening. This feel for the action and movement of the horse is further developed when the pupil rides trained horses which perform the movements correctly. Then to reinforce this practical education students at the Spanish Riding School also have to learn the anatomy of a horse and how it works.

Although there cannot be an exact schedule for the training of a rider an average apprentice will spend six months on the lunge, prior to any independent riding. It then takes two to four years for the rider to do High School movements, and another four to six years before the student can himself train horses to perform advanced work.

The training of the Lipizzaner starts when they are 3 years of age. It is divided into three stages of riding. These were established in writing in *The Directives for the Implementation of Methodical Procedure in the Training of Rider and Horse at The Imperial Spanish Riding School*. These were written in 1898 by Field Marshal Franz Holbein von Holbeinsburg, and chief rider Johan Meixner.

Before the riding starts, the horse, like the human student starts on the lunge. The stallions are lunged, using side reins attached directly on to a snaffle bit. The aim of this period of training is to achieve mental relaxation and physical co-ordination.

The lungeing is followed by the first phase of riding, which entails about six months of straightforward exercises. The purpose of this is to develop a natural equilibrium, to strengthen the muscles, and to increase responsiveness. Consequently much of the work is done on a loose rein and no tight turns are demanded.

The next phase covers a further one or two years of training. During this time the basic principles of a straight horse and one going forward must be confirmed and gymnastic exercises introduced. Colonel Handler liked the young horses to be ridden forward, to the limit that any further forwardness and they would lose their balance or go faster. He advocated achievement of true collection through increased impulsion. Too many people he said ignore this basic principle, and their 'collected' horse tends to drag hinds and lack the element of forwardness. Furthermore this forward tendency must originate from the hindquarters and go through the horse to produce an elastic, easy tension in the reins.

In the third or fourth year of training, horses enter the final phase when High School movements are introduced. By this time the stallions have been allotted their own particular rider. The horses are taught the Grand Prix dressage movements and the schools above the ground. The levade, capriole and courbette, which originated in the Middle Ages as useful tactics in war, are now used as exercises to make the horse and rider supple and to entertain the general public.

The schools above the ground and the development of the piaff, are taught largely through a speciality of the Spanish School, work in hand. This starts in the second year of training, but only the most skilled members are allowed to train their horses in this way. The horse is saddled and bridled, side reins attached and a cavesson with lead rein added. The trainer then works the horse with a wall on one side. The horse is familiarised with the whip and taught to recognise it as an aid rather than a means of punishment. Then the trainer, who is level with the forehand, asks the horse to go forward, tapping the hind fetlocks with the whip. The side reins are gradually shortened, and lowered, as the horse understands what is required of him. The benefit of this method of work is that without the weight of the rider it is easier for the horse to put his hind legs further under him. This helps to make his hips, knees and haunches more supple, so preparing him for collected work.

Another feature of the Spanish Riding School is the work between pillars. In the centre of the Winter Riding School stand two pillars, 5 feet apart and decorated with flags. No horse is attached to them until his third year at least and only after he has learnt the piaff with forward impetus. At this stage they can be used to achieve a more elevated piaff and the school jumps.

The Spanish Riding School's training programme results in the stallions enjoying long school life, some remain in work up to 20 years of their life. Occasionally this regular routine is broken by exercise in the Summer School, a small outside arena where the stallions can enjoy the treat of fresh air and sunshine. It must surprise some people how little of this they seem to need in order to lead a long, healthy and apparently contented life.

ADMINISTRATION AND COMPETITION

Austria's most impressive schools have won her international fame, but have helped her little in becoming a serious contender for equestrian competitive honours. It is the National Federation, the Bundesfachverband fur Reiten und Fahre in Osterreich, that has set about binding the various Austrian approaches together and stimulating interest in the previously rather exclusive activity of riding.

The headquarters are in Vienna and the officers oversee the work of the regional committees which have been set up in each of Austria's nine provinces. The Federation is beginning to exert more influence helped by a growing supply of funds as the government now gives them a grant and the racing tote, as in France, is generous towards all equestrian pastimes.

Money donated in this manner has been used to finance the training of the top show jumpers, who go on courses with Austria's sporting hero, Hugo Simon; the top dressage riders who go to Georg Wahl and the top event riders who go to Wahl and to the German, Pohlmann. Finance is also being directed towards training the young and with successful results. In 1974, Austria won the junior show jumping team European championship. At present, the parents of all children under 18 owning registered horses receive a small grant.

The FN also organises the major shows. Austria has become famous for its annual autumn show in Vienna. It is popular amongst competitors for both good courses and for the fun. It was the first international show to accentuate the amusement type classes (fancy dress jumping classes and the like), although Britain's Olympia show has now followed suit. Riders went to Vienna to enjoy themselves in such events as fancy dress competitions, as well as to win, and the crowd went to laugh as well as to be excited.

The Austrians are becoming increasingly serious about equestrian sports. In 1974 they staged their first CCIO at Luxenburg. Five nations fought out the Nations Cup but it was the Grand

Prix that made the home crowd happiest as it was won by their champion, Hugo Simon. These big shows, organised by the FN, offer good prize money, but there are very few of this standard. There are more, including events, where a little prize money is given, but for most of the year Austrians compete at small shows, organised by their clubs, where glory is the only reward. This does not deter competitors, for increasing numbers jump, event and perform dressage tests under these unremunerative terms.

In the past, Austria's equestrian reputation depended upon that small group from the Spanish Riding School, but today, increasing numbers are striving to win honours for their country. Expansion programmes are under way – to breed horses, build clubs, educate trainers, polish up competitors and improve the shows. Starting virtually from scratch the Austrians are benefiting from finding out how other European countries did, and are doing, it.

CHAPTER SEVEN

BRITAIN

THE aims, methods and pastimes of British horsemen have been very different from those of their counterparts across the Channel. The riders of the British Isles have been the leaders of the sporting approach, with hunting and steeplechasing being their metiers, rather than dressage and indoor riding. They learnt too by experience, by galloping and jumping and were suspicious, to the point of scorning, the scholastic approach of the Europeans who thought out how things should be done.

With the hunting field and racetrack being the most common schools of British equestrianism, it was boldness rather than method that taught people how to ride, individualism rather than uniformity that was fostered. It makes great competitors of riders, who have won many honours in show jumping and eventing, but no common style has emerged.

Today British riding is changing, for the massive post-war recruitment of riders has introduced people who have neither the opportunity, time or youth to learn by experience; they have to be taught, so riding schools have been built, riding clubs formed, riding instructors trained and employed to educate the new riders.

As in so many fields, British complacency in their traditional methods is being shaken. European schools have been found to yield some benefits that the sporting, individual methods did not. Consequently, the British are questioning and adjusting traditional approaches; opening their doors to the Continent with riding being improved by learning and thinking about it and not merely by experiencing it.

The U.K. is going through an exciting if occasionally confusing time as we appear to be merging with Europe not merely economically and politically, but also in the world of the horse. The result though, the tempering of natural horsemanship with a little thought, must be an improvement and augurs well for the future.

THE HORSE

Unlike developments in Europe, no breed of warmblood is being systematically developed in Britain for the fast growing world of competition and riding. Instead, the offshoots of breeds developed for other purposes, or crosses between them, are being utilised. With the wonderful equine blood of the British Isles even such a haphazard production has resulted in many great competition horses.

The best equine blood in the U.K. is the thoroughbred. It is the fastest and most valuable horse in the world. During the seventeenth and eighteenth centuries the British used systematic methods to develop this breed. They still devote endless thought, finance and experience in order to improve, or at least to maintain, standards.

Many of these thoroughbreds would make excellent horses for competition and riding, but usually the most suitable (that is those with substance, size and temperament) are just those wanted for racing and are consequently worth a great deal for this, the most remunerative of equestrian activities. Those with more reasonable price tags are all too often small, lack bone and have excitable temperaments. However, crossed with the more common breeds, these deficiencies can be eradicated and half-breds have been the most common British riding horse.

The breeders who produce Britain's riding horses are usually individuals whose breeding stock is often a retired hunter, jumper and so on and rarely a mare bought specifically for breeding. Most are half-bred mares with undocumented mixtures of ancestors which might include some Heavy Horse, Irish Draught, Cleveland, Hackney or even Welsh Cob.

The potential of the mare is rarely analysed – partly because without documents it is difficult to do so and partly because breeding is undertaken for the fun and the joy of seeing foals, rather than to breed the best possible horse. In addition it is commonly held in Britain that 'Good uns can't be bred – they're freaks'. Consequently matings are rarely thought about, the mare is taken off to the nearest stallion, though occasionally that 'freak' does get born.

One institution that, with the aid of a government grant, does help breeders of riding horses is the Hunter Improvement Society (HIS). Founded in 1885 they hold an annual stallion show where privately owned thoroughbred stallions are judged on their conformation. The best (60 to 70 entires) are awarded premiums on the condition that these stallions stand at a reduced fee. The aim is to bring good-class stallions within the financial range of more owners of mares.

The difference between this system and those in European countries is that the stallions are chosen with little account being taken of their movement and none of their temperament, performance ability and pedigree. It is another illustration of an excellent British system which needs some modernising, for the HIS was formed to encourage breeding of hunters and army horses. Choosing stallions on the basis of their conformation was adequate for these types because soundness and toughness were the most important qualities. But competitions, like racing, are more arduous and require an athlete whose production is more likely with systematic breeding.

Systematic breeding, the registration of stock and the keeping of pedigrees is necessary, but the British seem reluctant to promote such a system, for although the produce of the HIS premium stallions can be registered in the Hunter Stud Book, few owners bother to do so. Registration does mean little, however, with pedigrees only being given for one or two generations.

Some breeders aware of the shortcomings of the British system have gone to Europe to purchase Hanoverians, Trakehners and Dutch stallions that have been specifically developed for competitions and riding. These imports are in increasing demand, especially as they make such excellent crosses with the thoroughbred, injecting sensible temperaments, movement and substance. And they have pedigrees which makes a throwback unlikely.

The British riding horse, like its owners and riders, consists of a great variety of types. It does give vent to British individualism that riders can go show jumping on cobs, or thoroughbreds, or mixtures, but it does seem likely that a higher standard of horse could be more consistently produced if the British did not rely on 'freaks' and set out to produce a competition horse in the same way as they do racehorses.

RIDING CLUBS AND CENTRES

Britain's equestrian club system is very different from that in Europe. With sporting, independent minded riders it has been the hunt, not the club, that is the central feature of most riders' lives.

The most important network of clubs, the pony club, originated as attachments to hunts and were formed with the purpose of promoting hunting. The first branch was formed in 1929, it thrived and now there are about 300 branches with 50,000 members.

The idea of pony clubs spread overseas. Today there are more than 1,000 branches all over the world. The only area in which the idea did not take hold was in Europe, where most youngsters either joined vaulting associations, or became junior members of riding clubs.

The pony clubs were started by hunt minded folk, who wanted to foster a love of this sport amongst the young. Children's meets were held, and in the summer rallies organised, to improve the children's riding and their knowledge about the care of the horse. This education led to the formation of a graduated series of tests (A, B, C, D) and today the A certificate is a high enough qualification to ensure an excellent start to a professional career with horses.

Competitive pony club activities were only started in 1949 and were opposed by the 'true blue' British who thought it would endanger children's sporting spirit. Horse trials were the first venture and such is their success that there is hardly an international event rider who did not start as a member of their local pony club team.

Polo has been equally productive, for, since the introduction of the national championships in 1958, graduates include the best of the British players.

Most show jumpers also began riding with the pony clubs but it was only in 1971 that a national championship was started in this activity.

The pony club has thus developed into an educational channel for young British riders, but when they graduate (20 years of age maximum), relatively few join the riding club which fulfils a rather different role from both their counterparts in Europe and the pony club in the U.K.

The riding club is rarely based at a school where horses are kept or hired from, as in Europe; nor has it become a production line for top riders, but instead is a base for amateur equestrians. Most clubs are formed to provide some fun and a little education for like minded equestrian enthusiasts. The membership is dominated by the housewife and the weekend rider, and the activities provide valuable opportunities for the rider who has not the time, money or ability to join the circuit of more remunerative competitions.

The post-war riding boom has led to a vast increase in numbers of such riders and there has been a spectacular expansion of the riding club movement. This now consists of 400 clubs with nearly 20,000 members.

Most clubs hold small shows and events and there are qualifying rounds and a final for the national riding championships in eventing, jumping, dressage and prix caprilli. In addition to these valuable opportunities for the less experienced or able riders to compete, there are educational provisions. Rallies are held often with professional instructors; clinics and talk-ins are popular, and there is an examination system consisting of a series of riding club tests (Grades 1 to 4), which are of a similar standard to those for the pony club.

TRAINERS

The pony club and riding club tests are for the amateur. They do not examine candidates in their ability to teach, which is the role of the British Horse Society (BHS) examinations.

The easiest of these examinations is the one for the British Horse Society Associate Instructor Certificate (BHSAI). Nearly 2,000 candidates sat this examination in 1975, but less than 35% passed as being capable of looking after horses and instructing under supervision.

The next grade, an innovation in 1975, is the British Horse

Society Intermediate Instructor Certificate (BHSII). It was started because the third stage, the British Horse Society Instructor Certificate (BHSI), was so much more advanced than the BHSAI, that few horsemen (about 100 a year) progressed sufficiently to take this examination. A BHSI Certificate qualifies holders to teach, school horses and run a yard of horses.

The ultimate qualification in Britain is the British Horse Society Fellowship (FBHS), for which candidates must be a minimum of 25 years old and are examined in equitation and training the horse, ability as an instructor and capability in a discussion on equitation and training in all their branches.

This British equestrian educational system is not centred around a national school. Candidates do not have to partake in a specified course, or courses, like those run for the Scandinavians at Strömsholm, the Germans at Warendorf and for the French at Saumur. Instead they can obtain their education wherever they choose. As long as they have the necessary qualifications, such as four Ordinary level subjects in the General Certificate of Education for a BHSAI, or a BHSAI certificate before taking the BHSII they can present themselves on due notification, for examination at one of the BHS approved centres.

This decentralised educational system is a reflection of, and furthers, the individualistic approach to riding by the British. It suits the nature of the British rider that the system is not doctrinaire; that no particular style is hammered upon them and they know too that it is the best in the English speaking world. Many of the candidates for these examinations come from Australia, South Africa, Canada, and America in particular. The elite list of Fellows of the British Horse Society includes five from America and one from Canada.

With the large number of people from Britain and abroad wishing to qualify through the BHS system, more and more privately run schools are starting courses to prepare students for examinations. The most important of these are run by the Fellows of the BHS.

Brian Young

One of the most senior and distinguished of the British Fellows is Brian Young who runs his riding centre in historic and picturesque surroundings. Crabbet Park Equitation Limited lies in the grounds of the old Crabbet Arabian Stud – the first and most famous of the British Arabian studs – from which stock has been exported all over the world. Sadly the Arabian stock has now been dispersed and it is Brian Young's riding centre that is today upholding the equestrian tradition of this lovely Sussex Park.

Young started his centre in the mid-1960s when he retired as national instructor. That position had been something of a nomadic one. For five years he travelled the country educating amateur instructors. At Crabbet he has built a more permanent base, with two large indoor schools, outdoor arenas, cross-country courses and purpose built accommodation for sixty students and staff.

Although Brian Young is perhaps best known for his education of young professionals, his own varied education makes him proficient in many spheres. After service in the army during the war a three-month course at the renowned post-war civilian riding centre – Porlock Vale – led eventually to his becoming their chief instructor. This was followed by a spell in competition riding, including a ride around Badminton, some time at Lord Derby's stud, a period as instructor at the Silver Hound, before promotion to national instructor. Young is thus able to help students at his centre to prepare for competitions and they come for either week long courses, with accommodation provided, or for day or evening lessons. The proximity of the school to London means that many of his clients can use the classes held after normal working hours.

Young's professional courses are, however, the most international with students from America, Australia and Canada. They can choose a four month, or a one month, intensive course and they have school horses to ride, most of whom are capable of the medium movements of a dressage test.

Molly Sivewright

Brian Young gained his BHS Fellowship in 1961, the same year as Mrs. Molly Sivewright achieved the same distinction. Her establishment, Talland School of Equitation, is close to Cirencester in Gloucestershire and is again best known for training instructors.

A friendly atmosphere is promoted by Mrs. Sivewright who likes to think of Talland as being a large family. Horses are housed in boxes around every corner, laughter and running feet are continuously heard, yet everything happens on time and many activities are condensed into one day. Although Mrs. Sivewright smiles and jokes, her erect posture, her strong clear way of speaking give her an imposing air of authority which ensures that every plan she makes, every word she utters, is obeyed.

Her plans, however, are based on flexibility. Everybody possible is fitted in. Horse and rider combinations come for individual lessons, and intensive jumping, eventing, dressage and hunting courses are held.

Finns, Australians, Americans and New Zealanders come for long stays to prepare for competitive riding and for BHS Instructors' examinations, and British students wanting to take anything, from a BHSAI to a Fellowship, go to Talland to learn.

The school is a family concern. Colonel Charles Sivewright is the administrator and chief organiser and his mother-in-law, Mrs. Ryder Richardson, and his three daughters, all of whom have represented Britain in eventing or dressage, help with instruction.

The Sivewrights are competition minded which helps to give Talland a more youthful, modern and enthusiastic approach. It does mean, too, that they have to guard their amateur status for, as professionals, the opportunities to ride for Britain are very limited. Consequently Mrs. Sivewright and her three talented daughters only instruct on a part-time basis. They train the school's instructors and help competition riders as well as the local riding and pony club.

Much of the instruction at the school is carried out by professionals led by Miss Barbara Jupp, BHSI. Two trainers also pay regular visits to the school and these are Richard Stillwell and the Swedish dressage Olympic gold medallist, Major Boltenstern (see Sweden). The latter has had most influence on the Sivewrights' style of riding and his twice, or three times a year visits have instilled in the family a sympathetic approach to training the horse, with lightness as a major aim.

Major Boltenstern first instructed Mrs. Sivewright on a course organised by Colonel V. D. S. Williams. Colonel Williams is the man who did so much to introduce to England the value of riding classically rather than by mere intuition and experience alone. Williams set up a two-way education system, sending British instructors to Europe to learn and inviting well known Continental trainers to the U.K.

In Britain he created a headquarters for this education at Winkfield and called it the Centre of British Horsemanship. Sadly the British were not yet ready for such a serious Continental type training venture and did not give it enough support to keep this excellent project prosperous. Nevertheless, during its time of operation it was, in Molly Sivewright's words, 'a source of great inspiration to me'.

Molly Sivewright first went to the centre in 1947, on the first civilian instructors course. It was open to those who had passed their preliminary BHS instructors courses with honours. Molly Sivewright was the youngest of those to qualify.

It was on this course that she became aware of the problems facing the British. One instructor would tell her to use diagonal aids and another the very opposite – lateral. The course, she claimed, gave her an inquiring mind, a realisation of the importance of systematic training for instructors and riders, and started her on her quest to find out what was best; but it was also an indication of the problems facing British horsemen. The shortage of knowledge about classical training, the tendency to learn by experience, the lack of a strong central organisation furthering equestrian education meant that British trainers were usually self-taught, independent minded and too nationalistic to adopt Continental methods. Consequently, they used a great variety of ideas and pupils had to face the confusion of conflicting methods.

With no distinct British system to adopt, Molly Sivewright was far-sighted enough to learn from Major Boltenstern. Apart from his great ability as a rider he represented the Swedish school; a compromise between German and French ideas and one more likely to suit a Briton than either of the two extremes.

Mrs. Sivewright and Brian Young are leading examples of BHS Fellows. These, the most highly qualified of the British instructors, tend to specialise in the production of further instructors. The role of training the competitors, those riders who earn public glory, has been concentrated in the hands of the independent, and often unqualified, trainers. Many of these trainers are either European, or have chosen to get at least a part of their education from the Continent.

John Lassetter

The trainer who has spent a large part of his educational time abroad is John Lassetter. He did go through the BHS system, becoming a BHSI, but he sought broader horizons and took off for Europe on an educational tour which included spells at the Spanish Riding School, Reinstitut von Neindorff and Saumur.

The character which created such initiative shows in his face. Huge eyes dominate the appearance of this small, slight, dark haired young man. He is an extrovert who loves talking and the spectacular side of riding. He had planned to take up a career on the stage, but a holiday spent on a special riding course for senior pony club members with Brian Young converted him to an equestrian life.

The equestrian education which followed was varied and comprehensive. He worked his way up to become chief instructor first at Porlock Vale and then at Crabbet Park. He travelled around the schools of England, working under Robert Hall and Major Boltenstern. He went to learn about Continental methods at von Neindorff's establishment in Germany before starting his campaign to get to the most exclusive riding school in the world – Vienna. First he worked to have the opportunity to be tested. This he achieved and passed, but it took one and a half years of correspondence, telegrams and visits for him to actually enter the school.

In the fourteen months he spent there, Lassetter decided the best teachers were the horses. The members of the Spanish School's greatest talents lay in the education of the horses who in turn could teach the student.

John Lassetter also became aware that Spanish School education could not be applied in totum to all horses. Many thoroughbreds would boil over if ridden with the same domination, so he determined to examine other methods. The Cadre Noir, the upholders of the more spirited less specialised or disciplined French school were his next destination, and he spent four months with them. It must have been a stimulating contrast to come from a serious, routine minded school where collection was the fore-most aim, to the Cadre Noir with riders so full of vitality and for whom impulsion and extended movements were more important aims.

He thus provided himself with a very broadly based education which is unusual in the equestrian world where adherence to a group of principles and a consistent approach is more typical. Some say John Lassetter's broad minded approach is confusing. He claims that every way has a great deal to commend it and he can choose according to the temperament, ability and attitude of his horses and riders an appropriate correction or exercise. As long as he has the ability to choose wisely, then his approach must have much to commend it.

Circumstances, though, have directed John Lassetter more towards the Spanish School methods. Upon leaving Saumur he ran Reitzentrum Markhof, an international dressage school just forty-five minutes from the centre of Vienna, and which was modelled upon its illustrious neighbour, the Spanish Riding School.

When in 1976 John Lassetter returned to the U.K. he brought with him four Lipizzaners from the Spanish School and one from the former Imperial Stud of Lipizza. The five white stallions are now the revered residents of Porlock Vale – Britain's foremost school in the years just after the war.

During this era Tony Collings was its director and he collected under him a talented group of men fresh from the army and keen to improve Britain's horsemanship. Tragically this gifted trainer was killed in an air crash, but many of those under him, such as Dick Hern (the Queen's racehorse trainer) and Brian Young have distinguished themselves elsewhere. Porlock, however, lost a little of its prestige without him; perhaps with its new and unusual director it might regain its renown.

Under John Lassetter the school runs professional orientated courses which include long term ones for house students who work in the house in exchange for a free AI course, working pupils who pay only a small fee, and shorter fee paying courses of six months for those preparing for their BHSII, and of three months for the BHSAI. These courses are run according to the same pattern as many in the U.K.; but his specialist dressage courses are more unique. These fulfil an important need in the U.K. for his trained Lipizzaner stallions can give pupils the feel of the movements which should help them when they come to train their own horses. Only riders that have established a classical position and have an idea of lateral work are accepted. They then spend some time on the lunge each day, in addition to riding horses that are proficient in varying fields. One stallion can do courbettes well, others piaff and passage, and then there are the younger and less advanced horses who can give pupils an idea of the intermediate levels of training.

As yet most of the students on these courses have come from Austria, France, U.S.A., and amongst the British it has been the youngsters, the 17-year-olds, who have been the most frequent pupils.

John Lassetter, however, does not want the school to become too specialised. He likes variety so he runs hunting weekends with lodgings and horses provided, and days arranged with the Staghounds and/or the Harriers. He likes too dramatics, and exhibitions are organised to include pas seul, quadrilles and pas de deux with his wife side saddle, and commentaries to music.

John Lassetter practises very different methods from the traditional British riders. He approaches riding more as an art than a sport, and teaches it through a series of logical steps rather than by acquirement of natural experience.

Richard Stillwell

Probably the best representative of a British school of training is Richard Stillwell. He looks very British, dons a drooping moustache and is rarely without a trilby or flat cap. He has that British knack of turning everything into 'sport', driving fast cars, enjoying jokes, playing pranks on pupils and friends and would set aside everything if he was offered a good day's foxhunting.

His equestrian education came originally from his father who was a well known horseman producing successful hacks, hunters and driving horses. Stillwell followed this up with extensive experience of hunting, riding point-to-point horses, going show jumping, eventing and showing – and talking to everyone.

Although his knowledge comes mainly from experience, in 1956

he did go on a concentrated six-month course with the Commandant Austen Smith. This Irish trainer had been a pupil at the homes
of classical jumping, the Italian cavalry schools of Pinerolo and
Tor de Quinto, so he was able to pass on their ideas to Stillwell.

Stillwell's lessons conform to no pattern, but appear to be
spontaneous affairs when serious education is tempered with a
good deal of fun. He directs his mischievous sense of humour
at his pupils, producing anything from laughter to tears; but
this is all part of his teaching method. The bumptious and over
confident are brought to earth and made to listen, while the nervous
and tense are boosted and relaxed.

Stillwell's pupils are not subjected to drastic changes in their
riding, merely adjustments, the aim is to bring out what he
believes are the basic qualities of a horseman – good balance,
seat and hands, but not to lay down hard and fast rules about the
details (i.e. length of stirrup, position of hands, etc.). It is too
easy, he says, to destroy what is already there and to take away
that vital confidence in their own ability.

The horses, however, have more radical treatment. He wants
suppleness, obedience and rhythm from them and is a maestro
at discovering a problem which inhibits these. He likes to ride
the horse and to find out for himself the difficulties. He says
'The horse has a simple language of telling me where the problem
is'. This is his gift – being one of the few people to understand a
language which is felt, not heard.

He finds the most common cause of problems is in the mouth.
Although a horse, properly broken, should never need more than
a snaffle, accidents and/or lack of knowledge all too often
put an end to this ideal. Stillwell usually subjects such cases to
a bitting session when all shapes, sizes and textures are tried in
the mouth until the horse is happier.

Flexibility and innovation are the basis of the Stillwell system.
He has no formula to work to but seeks out problems and tries
to provide an answer. He says there is an answer to everything,
with the proviso that a horse cannot be worked out of a problem
when he is physically incapable, either through injury or im-
maturity.

Stillwell's ability in finding quick answers, rather than con-
forming to classic principles and of adapting existing assets

rather than starting again, means improvements are made quickly and existing systems are not unduly disturbed. It means that a few days under Richard Stillwell produce great changes in a horse and rider combination and, as a consequence, he has become one of the most popular teachers of courses in the world. He travels regularly to Greece, Holland, France, Canada and Ireland, in addition to nearly every area of Britain. Nor are these courses confined to the top-class riders, for Richard Stillwell wants everybody, whatever their ability and time available, to enjoy riding. He holds a great variety of courses, ranging from those for hunting enthusiasts, members of riding clubs, young riders on scholarships at Britain's National Equestrian Centre to those for adult international show jumpers and eventers.

Stillwell's star pupils, however, normally come for individual lessons at his stables at Hand Post Farm in Berkshire. Pupils include the Olympic triple gold medallist Richard Meade, European event champion Lucinda Prior Palmer, World event champion Mary Gordon Watson and European show jumping champion Ann Backhouse. However, due to the increasing popularity of his courses Stillwell spends fewer and fewer days at home.

Most of his teaching time is spent in strange schools, but this has meant that a large and great variety of riders have spent a few days under him. It has given them a glimpse of the concept of a British school of riding where 'sport' is encouraged, confidence and dash are thought to be vital, improvements are made by adjustments and gadgetry is not spurned if it avoids fights and produces quicker results. The adherence to fixed principles and methods is avoided, because of the fear that to do so could destroy the essential spark of character and ability within horse and rider.

Lars Sederholm

Lars Sederholm, who runs a thriving riding centre in Oxfordshire, favours methods based on established principles. He, like the famous American trainer Bertalan de Nemethy, thinks his pupils are happier, and better off, working according to clearly established methods towards a defined goal.

Sederholm is reluctant to adapt the existing styles of pupils but prefers to get them to accept a wholesale adoption of what he calls the 'Waterstock system'. He is however, like all good trainers, a psychoanalyst and according to the temperament and ability of his pupils uses different ways of getting this across.

It is a system which he himself has devised and he is particularly well qualified to do so. He was born and brought up in Sweden, where they use an open minded and sensible approach to riding, gleaning the most suitable styles and methods of riding from the rest of the world. Sederholm's family were successful business people and not remotely horsey. His natural riding talent (he was the British three-day event champion for three consecutive years) came from an unknown ancestor, but he did also inherit a business man's brain. It has given him the ability to learn, think and plan which puts him in a different class to most members of the equestrian world.

Consequently, after his experiences as travelling assistant to the Olympic quadruple dressage gold medallist St. Cyr and as an apprentice with Mrs. Joan Gold in Britain, and with the benefit of taking courses and clinics all over the world, he put together his general pattern of training for the education of horse and rider. This is based on all round horsemanship. He believes that even specialists can benefit from the experience of other activities and the knowledge of all aspects of the horse, from feeding to lungeing. For example, at his school at Waterstock, close to Oxford, show jumpers go over cross-country fences, dressage riders go show jumping and so on.

The Waterstock Equestrian Centre is based around the Georgian house occupied by Lars Sederholm and his wife Diana. The house is wedged between training arenas, an indoor school and blocks of stables built in different styles and at irregular intervals. These are used nowadays to accommodate the ever increasing number of students who want Sederholm's services. All types of students come, most bringing their own horses, as there are only a few retired eventers to act as school horses, and the young ones being trained on for sale. Many students choose to come as working pupils, in order to save money. Others pay to join the intensive courses covering the Waterstock system and then there are preparatory courses for the BHS examinations.

It is in the field of competition, however, that Waterstock is best known. There are four day preparatory courses for events and jumping, in addition to individual lessons. Students come from all over the world and the British include many of the best riders in the land, such as Caroline Bradley and Graham Fletcher, who come for brush-up sessions, and other like Chris Collins who use it as a permanent base.

With such a large number of pupils, Lars Sederholm needs assistance and his main help comes from Richard Walker, the 1969 Badminton winner, and Gill Watson BHSI, a winner of the Burghley three-day event in 1969. Sederholm himself can only take a limited number of pupils, but he holds daily meetings between pupils and tutors in order to keep in touch. He also likes to walk in and check up on lessons. His presence sharpens the atmosphere for he imposes his enthusiasm, his driving personality and his clear methods on any equestrian student.

In his logical manner he thought he could help both his students and his income if he found them the right type of horses on which to practise his methods. This has resulted in him becoming a horse dealer. He acts as an agent between buyers and sellers all over Britain, Europe and America and he has a store of high-class 3-year-olds and over, which are given a basic training, according to his methods, in preparation for their sale.

Lars Sederholm has thus built up at Waterstock a set pattern of riding to follow, courses or lessons in all aspects of riding and horses which can be bought as suitable partners on which to practise his principles.

Robert Hall

There is only one other trainer in the U.K. who can rival Lars Sederholm's ability to plan logically and efficiently and to earn himself a due financial reward in the process, and that is Robert Hall. There is, however, little competition between them, for they specialise in different fields; Hall in dressage, Sederholm in jumping and eventing.

Robert Hall, dark haired and good looking, is married to a blonde, pretty Dutch-born lady called Yook. She is an Olympic dressage rider and a top judge (becoming in Montreal the first lady to judge Olympic dressage). Hall himself is Britain's most successful dressage trainer and numbers amongst his disciples leading administrators and riders. The Halls' influence and ability is such that they are close to holding British dressage in the palms of their hands.

Robert Hall developed his first school at Fulmer in Buckinghamshire, but it prospered to such an extent that he opened two more in Edinburgh and Yorkshire. The feature of these three schools is that they own some of the best trained school horses in the country. There are 170 in all, including some Lipizzaners. Robert Hall has even spread his domain to America, opening a school in Boston. Here there are, however, only six school horses, as the school's speciality is to train horse and rider combinations.

In all the Hall schools, the Fulmer system is taught; a system which is the same for all horses and riders and for every activity. The only differences are that although the stages are identical and worked through in the same order, firstly the final levels differ and a racehorse, for example, will be trained to a much easier stage than a dressage horse; and secondly, because horses and riders differ in temperament, physique and ability adjustments have to be made as to the rate of progress and how the aims are asked for. Consequently, a lazy horse will have to be chivied up and excited, a highly strung horse calmed down and given confidence in order to get them both to the same stage.

The Fulmer system has been derived from Hall's personal experience and logic. A major influence has been the principles of the Spanish School where Hall was himself a pupil. He has not, however, carried out a wholesale adoption of these principles as they were devised for horses and riders that thrived on discipline and demanding methods. In Britain many thoroughbreds and civilians prosper better on coaxing and encouragement so Hall likes to make his training more like a discussion than a series of demands. The trainer asks a question and the pupil (human or equine) gives an answer. Nothing is asked which is too difficult for that stage or in any way against nature. The Fulmer system is an antithesis to anything artificial and to most circus riding, which when Robert Hall started teaching in the 1950s was what the British commonly thought of as dressage. It is a system which shuns the idea of forcing a horse to come on quickly, and it needs time and patience to follow.

Many of the principles of the Fulmer system are not merely different, but are frequently opposite to those more generally accepted. He takes pride in this originality, pointing out and accentuating rather than minimising differences and claims that variations in methods are much greater in the horse business than in any other sports. At first this might seem an odd approach when the general trend is to harmonise and minimise differences, but it is an excellent teaching aid, for comparisons and accentuation of extremes must help to clarify to the pupils what he wants to achieve.

Robert Hall expounds his principles in a forthright, logical and authoritative manner which communicates to his pupils the confidence to believe that his ideas are right. He adopts too an open minded manner making logic his 'god' and giving everyone the opportunity to question his ideas; but as yet he has always found the answers.

His goal for horse and rider is controlled relaxation, both mental and physical, for which the major ingredients are suppleness, flexibility, impulsion and balance. Arguments have raged in the British equestrian press about the viability of this concept, but it seems that critics base their arguments on a misunderstanding, taking relaxation to lead to a lack of impulsion. As Hall points out, these critics have not noticed the word control, which changes the whole nature of the relaxation.

Many of the British question, too, his ban on gadgetry; but he supports this with his aim of keeping the horse's paces and outline natural. He points out that a head held artificially in place means the rest of the body must become contorted and cannot operate with looseness and suppleness. It is only when the rider is not good enough to convey his wishes to the horse that gadgetry helps. Hall prefers to set about making right the rider's inadequacies, to make gadgets superfluous rather than to start pulling the horse about.

The principle that has gained Hall the largest number of critics is that the rider's seat should not be used to push the horse forward or to activate the hind legs. A heavy seat, he claims, has the opposite effect, for it makes a horse go hollow and so prevents the hind legs from coming under the body.

He says, as for all his ideas, that he would relinquish this controversial concept of the effect of the rider's seat if anyone can use logic to prove him wrong. As yet, no one has and as he said if the system is wrong 'We are extremely busy'.

As Robert Hall's doctrines are different, or even opposite, to many schools, his students have to be devotees for it is difficult to combine a smattering of his teaching with a little of someone else's. Perhaps though this contributes to his influence. He does get the entire attention of his pupils, he does provide them with a clear path and, however different the course of the path, it does produce a winning end product. At the 1976 Olympics he had a pupil on the team, Diana Mason, with Special Edition and another in the reserves, Lady Joicey with Pussycat.

David Hunt

The young trainer offering a challenge to Robert Hall's supremacy in the British dressage world is David Hunt. His school, Gracious Pond Stables at Chobham in Surrey, provides an alternative for pupils which is different in atmosphere, approach, methods and principles. There are no indoor schools, or smart facilities and although there is a large sand arena much of the time is spent riding in the fields or on Chobham Common. The smart trimmings, the large-scale organisation are not Hunt's means of training. He uses nature and common sense, rather than logic and impressive facilities. He uses the continually changing circumstances of outdoor work to create impulsion and test that control over the horse is complete and not dependent on anything untoward occurring. This approach brings out problems rather than avoiding them, which is Hunt's intention. A horse, closeted in an indoor school, is less likely to do something unexpected than one outdoors.

David Hunt, however, has assets enabling him to face up to, and even use problems for he is an exceptionally talented rider and has that all devouring determination to succeed. He gets on a horse without a predetermined plan, to work it through stage one and progress to stage two, but only to feel what is needed. He might start such advanced work as a flying change on a novice horse if he feels this would help to get stage one correct.

It is a non-conformist school, one that has been established through 'finding out for myself'. David Hunt has worked under

Alison Oliver, but has found that riding horses and experimenting with them was a better way of getting an education than through people or books. Nor has he been to Continental schools, but he has spent hours watching riders at shows in Europe where he has been as a representative on Britain's dressage team. He has seen there, more than in Britain, the end products he is looking for in his training, rhythm, cadence and elasticity. He wants, too, to develop spring, an indication of contained power.

David Hunt trains his riders largely through the horse, as he believes that if he can get the horse to work correctly then the rider finds it easier to sit well and to apply the right aids. Consequently, a lesson at Gracious Pond usually consists of David Hunt riding the pupil's horse for three-quarters of the time and in the remaining part getting the pupil to feel what he wants of them. He has a knack of explaining personally and very vividly what is needed, for his knowledge comes from experience and thought rather than regurgitation of the ideas of other people.

The flaw in such a system, which has aims but no fixed methods, is that it depends on David Hunt's personal direction and riding. Delegation can only be limited, but this is of benefit to pupils, as they are not palmed off on substitutes. They receive David Hunt's personal and enthusiastic teaching of how to get their horse to work 'with' rather than 'for' them.

Hunt has met with great success and after only two years of running an idependent centre with his partner, the international dressage rider, Andrew Rymill, he has a growing clientele which includes the European adult and junior three-day event champions, Lucinda Prior Palmer and Venetia Salmond. He often has, too, horses which are trained and can give pupils a feel of advanced movements. It has resulted in him receiving students from America, but his speciality remains horse and rider combinations, which come to him for individual lessons, or are boarded at his stables.

David Hunt has introduced refreshing elements to British dressage. A highly competitive spirit and a desire to utilise and bring out character rather than to subdue it, an awareness that the obedience he demands from his horse must be tempered with vitality, cadence and excitement, not merely quietness.

Daniel Pevsner

Another young dressage orientated trainer in Britain, is
Daniel Pevsner, but his approach is more scholastic and less competitive minded than David Hunt's. Although an Israeli, his
basic equestrian education was gained at British schools, and at
Robert Hall's and Molly Sivewright's in particular.

In 1971 he became one of the youngest to earn a Fellowship
of the British Horse Society and soon after this set off to gain as
much information as possible from the world's greatest schools
and trainers. He spent time with von Neindorff in Germany,
but his longest spell was with the Portuguese maestro, Oliveira.
He interrupted his apprenticeship there to receive some contrasting education with the Cadre Noir at Saumur, and completed his
Continental education by becoming one of the very rare pupils
at the Spanish Riding School.

Daniel Pevsner is a person who has relied on his intelligence
more than natural riding talent to make his way in the equestrian
world. It means that having had to learn how to do it himself
he is particularly good at putting across to pupils how they should
do it. Also his intellectual approach towards riding has enabled
him to absorb a great deal at the famous schools of learning that
he has attended.

Pevsner now has his base in Buckinghamshire, where an
increasing number of pupils go as enthusiasm gathers momentum
for his quiet scholastic type training based on an unusually broad
and thorough education.

Alison Oliver

A feature in Britain, unlike the rest of Europe, is that female
riders outnumber men. They are also able to hold their own in
competition against them.

No other country could challenge a British ladies' eventing or
jumping team and British ladies were the first to ride in Olympic
show jumping, first to win a jumping medal, to win an Olympic
gold medal, to win a European three-day event championship
title and to win a World individual title. There is no question
that men have to accept the best of the ladies as their equals in
equestrian competitions.

As trainers, however, no lady has risen to the top of the tree.

There are quite a large number who are Fellows of the BHS, Pat Manning has had success in training the junior dressage riders, but it is Alison Oliver, a pretty housewife and mother of two, who comes nearest to challenging the men in this sphere.

Alison Oliver has worked her way up from the bottom rung of the ladder, her big break coming when she joined the international dressage rider, Mrs. Joan Gold's equestrian centre at Warfield in Berkshire. There she rode and trained, and graduated to run the Warfield centre herself. Alison Oliver's leap to fame came when HRH Princess Anne adopted her as trainer and she was able to give this busy lady enough assistance to make her the individual European three-day event champion.

The keynote in Alison Oliver's training is individual attention which presupposes a relatively small set-up. At one time this was dominated by royal horses, but now that marriage has led to Princess Anne having her own yard, Alison Oliver has room for less regal pupils.

Having started as a trainer of horses rather than riders she used to help the riders by getting the horse going correctly and then sitting them on top; but with experience she found this usually only produced results in the short term. For lasting improvements the riders had to learn how to train the horses themselves, so now she only likes to ride in order to get to know the horses and their problems, and then to be able to relate them to her pupils so that they can work at it for themselves.

The most important aim for Alison is to get both the horse and rider in balance. The horse carrying himself and the rider not interfering with this self-balance. The horse must settle to accept the control of the hand and leg, yet at the same time must not rely on them to maintain a pace.

For the rider Alison said 'The art of riding is self analysis'. The rider must become aware of any loss of balance and be able to analyse their own reactions, so that they can make corrections.

Alison Oliver has the assistance of her husband, Alan, who is one of Britain's most famous show jumpers. His ideas, though, are somewhat less orthodox for he became famous in the 1940s and 1950s for his unique style of throwing himself into the air over a fence in order to take the weight off the horse's back. Combinations and closely related fences made this rather disturbing approach no longer feasible, so Alan, in the 1960s, had to carry out moderations and no longer hurls himself into the air over fences. He does still practise, however, precision jumping – holding a horse back until he sees a stride and then pushing on, rather than a flowing classical approach. Together this couple must give their pupils some interesting ideas.

Bertie Hill

There are more trainers who, in keeping with the nature of their countrymen, have an individual approach and suit the needs of very different pupils. In the West Country there is Bertie Hill, one of the few trainers who was a leading competitor and won an Olympic gold medal in the British team at the 1956 three-day event. He is inclined towards the more British approach, no rigid system, but an all round education with the maximum possible experience. He likes his pupils to go racing, hunting, jumping, eventing and to become competent horsemen. He likes too, in a similar fashion to Richard Stillwell, to bring out ability, to improve natural assets, rather than to apply doctrine. In order to achieve this Bertie Hill likes his pupils to come for a long stay and to bring their own horses.

The National Equestrian Centre

Britain's National Equestrian Centre is set in the midst of the Royal Agricultural Society's showground, on Lord Leigh's Stoneleigh estate, in Warwickshire. It consists of a large indoor school, a range of office buildings, stables, outdoor arenas and cross-country fences. There is no national trainer in overall charge of the centre. The British had awarded this title to various eminent trainers during the 1950s and 1960s, but the post has never been a success. The independent, individual British riders have very definite and very different ideas as to how to ride in their various sports. Disturbances and misunderstandings were the usual outcome of trying to make them adopt the ideas of a particular trainer. The administrators have accepted this trait in their countrymen, which is, after all, also an asset as it nurtures the will to win. They now give riders grants to train under whosoever they please.

The National Equestrian Centre instead of becoming a base

for a national trainer, is developing into a University of the Horse. The best instructors from all over Britain and the rest of the world, including such eminent people as Gunnar Andersen, Bertalan de Nemethy and Jack le Goff have held clinics there. Top competitors and instructors, with their own horses, are invited to join these short courses which specialise in dressage, eventing, jumping or instruction according to who is giving the course.

After a period of experimentation the National Equestrian Centre has found its role. It has become, not a routine school with a set pattern of education, but more of a conference centre providing the gilt, the opportunity for the insular and widely scattered British to have an introduction to the ideas of the world's best instructors. They can go away and adopt them, or not, at will; they are free to keep their notorious individualism and independence.

ADMINISTRATION AND COMPETITION

In Britain the world of competition is overseen by the British Equestrian Federation. Their offices are at the National Equestrian Centre. The Federation has two major branches, one the British Show Jumping Association (BSJA) is in control of Britain's most lucrative equestrian sport, show jumping and, the other, the British Horse Society (BHS) oversees pony clubs, riding clubs, riding schools approvals system, eventing, dressage, examinations, endurance riding and so on. The BSJA, and each of the various sections of the BHS, are relatively independent units although the advantages of economies of scale is leading to some integration. It is still not sufficient though, to have an overall registration of horses, owners and riders as in Germany. Instead each section, BSJA, dressage and the like, have their own members and each horse and rider has to be registered with each and every one of the sections under which it wishes to compete.

Grading too varies, from show jumping when it depends on financial earnings, to dressage where it is based on points. The system is symptomatic of the British people's fierce independence and dislike of uniformity. It nurtures, too, much stronger divisions between equestrian sports than is the case in Europe. In Britain riders tend to stick to their sports, to be so proud of their particular activity that they are disdainful of all others, which all too often excuses them of ever trying their hand at anything else. Trainers, like Lars Sederholm, who believe in all round horsemanship, may help to break down the barriers, but it will not be easy. Apart from the participants' fierce confidence that their sport is the best, there is also a tendency for very different characters to practise the three major activities.

Show jumping is the world of the professional, the showman, the highly competitive spirit and the new rich; eventing, that of the amateur, the old fashioned, the sporty, dashing and country minded; dressage of the quiet, the devotees and the artistic minded.

Participants in one feel outsiders in another, not merely because of their lack of knowledge of it, but also because of the lack of similar characters.

Show jumping

Television exposure has turned show jumping into a national sport. With television ratings second only to soccer, television companies pay big money to cover show jumping and sponsors pay equally big money to get their names on the screen as donators of prize money, owners of horses and so on. Competitors demand big prize money as their due, believing themselves the cause of all this national interest. Since the Second World War, show jumping has developed, from a rather amateurish affair, into an industry.

It has become an occupation for the top participants who lead a nomadic existence in order to compete at the shows offering the best prize money. Some have developed into television personalities. For example, Ted Edgar the bawdy comedian, Harvey Smith the defier of authority, David Broome the down to earth Welshman. Many too, can earn good incomes from advertising, riding horses for sponsors, selling horses for vast sums, training riders and, in the case of Harvey Smith, even singing songs and selling T-shirts.

The attraction to the general public of show jumping is, partly, its colourful participants who range from the intelligent and classic riders, like Caroline Bradley, to the provocative, rough tacticians like Ted Edgar; and partly the success of the riders. The British can be very proud of their countrymen who compete on equal terms with the riders from any other country. David Broome and Marion Mould have won World championships; Ann Moore, David Broome and Peter Robeson Olympic individual medals; Paddy McMahon, Pat Smythe, Ann Backhouse, Sue Welsh, Anneli Drummond Haye, David Barker and David Broome European titles. The adult teams have won the President's Cup (the World team championship) more times than any other country and British juniors have dominated the role of honour for the European team championships.

It is a great record, only lacking Olympic gold medals. These have proved elusive since 1952, when Britain's team victory at Helsinki and Harry Llwellyn's success with Foxhunter first aroused public interest in the sport and started it on its road to the public fame of today.

Eventing

Eventing is also gaining enormous public support, with vast crowds attending and even more people watching on their televisions such competitions as the two major three-day events, held at Badminton and Burghley. This sort of popularity is due, in part, to the success of Princess Anne and to her parents who are such great supporters; also to the glories the British competitors have won. Team and individual Olympic gold medals were theirs in 1972 and the team won the gold in both 1956 and 1968.

Since the inauguration of the European championships in 1953 the British have won eight out of thirteen team championships and one out of two World championships. They have also earned one individual World championship title, with Mary Gordon Watson in 1970, plus eight individual European championships. It is a record that no other nation can boast of.

Spectators at events have the satisfaction of watching some of the greatest competitors in the world and have the pleasure of wandering through some of the loveliest parks and grounds in Britain. Events have developed into an activity held at stately homes and nearly all of the sixty-, one-, two- and three-day events held during the spring and autumn seasons are set in superb surroundings. The number of events staged is very many more than in any other country giving the British the best possible competitive opportunities.

The other advantage the British have in eventing is that their equestrian traditions of hunting and racing stand them in good stead in this sport. Their natural bold equestrian upbringing has made such riders as Richard Meade, Hugh Thomas, Lucinda Prior Palmer and Mark Phillips masters of the cross-country section.

Combined driving

A new booming equestrian sport is combined driving. Like eventing it has the benefit of royal patronage, for HRH The Duke of Edinburgh retired from the polo field to take up driving. It was natural for him to promote his new sport and, as President of the FEI, he was able to play a major role in the drawing up of rules and getting competitions going both in Britain and internationally.

Like eventing, combined driving has become a sport held in the parks of Britain's stately homes, which, together with the spectacular nature of the sport and the distinguished participants taking part, has led to great interest from spectators.

At Lowther in the Lake District, thousands turn out to see competitors in single, pair and team championships. Cirencester National Championships and Hickstead with the British Driving Derby are also popular events.

The British are proving to be good at this sport for, with Continental championships only having started in 1971, they have already a World team title and individual medals to their name.

Dressage

Increasing numbers of the British are being converted to this sport of Europeans. Event riders previously forced to do dressage in order to compete across country, have developed into dressage enthusiasts. Some who include Diana Mason, the first girl to ride in an international three-day event, have gone on to be competitors at Olympic Games standard. Others, who went to trainers and were made to do dressage before going jumping, also became keen and the dressage group membership has escalated to 2,000 (cf. 3,000 in eventing) and there were over 70 contests in 1976. Riders are also distinguishing themselves in international classes, with Jennie Loriston Clarke and Sarah Whitmore both winning in 1975 at this level.

It is still, however, Britain's weak spot in the equestrian sphere. The road to improvement must be by learning from the best. The British show jumpers raised their standards by educating themselves in Europe. Our competitors went to Europe – Pat Smythe and Harry Llwellyn our first great internationals spent a large part of their early career competing in Europe rather than in Britain; our course builders went to Europe – Pamela Carruthers the first British person to excel at an international level learnt much of her trade from Europeans; our show directors went to Europe – Douglas Bunn modelled his showground at Hickstead upon European ventures. It seems the British dressage riders will have to learn, like the show jumpers, from their masters – the Germans, French, Austrians, Swiss, Danes and Swedes. They can, like the Swedes and Swiss, sift from the horsemen in Europe the methods, ideas and approaches which suit them and their horses the best. The knowledge is in Europe for the taking, all that is needed is the enterprise to seek it out, and the will to work to apply it.

In dressage, the most artistic and scholastic sphere of horsemanship, the British have much to learn, but in other activities – hunting, jumping, eventing and the like, the Continentals can learn much from the British. As international barriers break down with the increasing ease of travel, there are more and more opportunities to find out and exchange knowledge; such and inter action must be of benefit to horsemanship everywhere. Let us make the most of it.

FRANCE

BREEDING

FEDEL, Federation Francais des Syndicate d'Eleveurs de Chevaux de Selle, 15 Rue Dumont d'Urville, Paris 16e.

Haras de St. Lo, BP 71 – 50010, Sant Lo, and Haras le Pin, 61310, Exmes (the most important studs for the Selle Français).

Haras de Pompadour, 19230 Arnac Pompadour (the most important stud for Arabs and Anglo-Arabs).

PURCHASING

Chambre Syndicale de Commerce de Chevaux de France, 51 Rue Dumont d'Urville, Paris 16e.

INSTRUCTION

Syndicat des maitres de Manege, (riding instructors), 27 Rue Chaveau, Neuilly sur Seine.

Fédération Francais des Sports Equestre, (riding schools), 164 Fauborg St. Honoré, Paris 75008.

ANTE, Association Nationale du Tourisme Equestre, (tourism on horseback), 12 Rue du Parc Royal, Paris 3e.

Loisirs Equestres Wagon Lits, (equestrian holidays), 14 Bd. des Capucines, 75009 Paris.

Club Mediterranée, (all disciplines), Centre equestre de Formation Specialisée, Domaine de la Noaille, Arnac Pompadour.

Académie Equestre, (dressage), Romilly sur Aigre (Eure et Loire) Tel: 24 à Romilly.

Academie Equestre de Touraine, (dressage), Domaine de Fonti-ville, Veigne (Indre et Loire).

College d'Equitation de l'Orchere, (all disciplines, including polo), Notre Dame d'Allençon (Main et Loire).

Ecole d'Equitation de Luzarches, (all disciplines, visits to studs, training centres and race meetings), Luzarches (Val d'Oise).

COMPETITIONS

Fédération Français des Sports Equestre, 164 Fauborg St. Honoré, Paris 75008.

GENERAL INFORMATION

Comité d'Information et de Promotion de Cheval, 51 Rue Dumont d'Urville, Paris 16e.

GERMANY

BREEDING

Hauptverband fur Zucht und Prufung deutscher Pferde e.V., (central organisation), D 4410 Warendorf, Lonsstrasse 13, Postfach 640.

Verband der Zuchter des Holsteiner Pferdes (Holsteins), 22 Elmshorn, Klostersande 93.

Verband Hannoverscher Warmblutzuchter e.V. (Hanoverians), 3 Hannover, Johannssenstrasse 10.

Westfalische Pferdestammbuch (Westfalians), 44 Munster (Westf), Engelstrasse 52.

PURCHASING

Breed Associations, as above.

INSTRUCTION

Deutsche Reiterliche Vereinigung, D 4410 Warendorf, Lonsstrasse 13, Postfach 640.

Reinstitut von Neindorff, 75 Karlsruhe, Nancystrasse 1.

Westfalische Reit- und Fahrschule (courses in driving as well as dressage and show jumping), 4400 Munster, Steinfurter Str. 103.

Deutsche Reitschule, 4410 Warendorf, Gestutstrasse 17.

COMPETITIONS

Deutsche Reiterlich Vereinigung, 4410 Warendorf, Gestutstrasse 17.

APPENDIX III

SWEDEN

BREEDING

Flyinge National Stud, Malmö, Skåne.

PURCHASING

Avlesforeningen, Svenska Varmbodiga Hasten, Bengt Bomqvist, Stora Ekered, 523 00 Ulricehamn.

INSTRUCTION

Ridframjandet, Bragevagen 12, 114 24 Stockholm.

COMPETITIONS

Svenska Ridsportens Centralforbund, Bragevagen 12, 114 24 Stockholm.

APPENDIX IV

SWITZERLAND

BREEDING

Haras Fédéral, CH – 1580 Avenches.

PURCHASING

Horse Auctions, Haras Fédéral CH – 1580 Avenches.

INSTRUCTION

Association Suisse des Professionnels de l'Equitation et Propriétaires de manèges, Case Postale 37, CH – 2532 Macolin.

COMPETITIONS

Schweizerischer Verband fur Pferdesport, Blankweg 70, Postfach, 3072 Ostermundigen, Berne.

DENMARK

BREEDING

Danish Sportshorse Breeding Association, 3 Vester Farimagsgade, 1606 Copenhagen V. Tel. (01) 14 36 88.

Oldenbuger, Frederiksburger, Norwedian Fjordhorse, Landsudvlget for Hesteavl, 3 Vester Farimagsgade, 106 Copenhagen V.

PURCHASING

Danish Sportshorse Breeding Association, 3 Vester Farimagsgade, 1606 Copenhagen V.

INSTRUCTION

Danish Riding Federation, Idraettens Hus, 2600 – Glostrup. Tel. (01) 45 55 55.

COMPETITIONS

Danish Riding Federation, Idraettens Hus, 2600 – Glostrup.

AUSTRIA

BREEDING

Bundeshangstenstallamt Stadl-Paura, Linz.

PURCHASING

Bundeshangstenstallamt Stadl-Paura, Linz.

INSTRUCTION

Bundesfachverband fur Reiten Und Fahren in Ostereich, A- 1040 Wien, Prinz-Eugen-Strasse 12/111, Haus des Sports.

COMPETITIONS

Bundesfachverband fur Reiten Und Fahren in Ostereich, A- 1040 Wien, Prinz-Eugen-Strasse 12/111, Haus des Sports.

BRITAIN

BREEDING

Hunter Improvement Society, National Westminster Bank Chambers, 8 Market Square, Westerham, Kent.

Cleveland Bay Horse Society, R. Stephenson, Esq., 20 Castlegate, Yorks.

PURCHASING

Hunter Improvement Society, address as above.

British Bloodstock Agency, 26 Charing Cross Road, London, W.C.2.

INSTRUCTION

Horsemanship and Examinations Committee, National Equestrian Centre, Kenilworth, War., CV8 2LR.

Association of British Riding Schools, Chesham House, Green End Road, Sawtry, Huntingdon, Cambs., PE17 5UY.

Waterstock Equestrian Centre, Waterstock, Nr. Oxford, Oxon.

Fulmer School of Equitation, Fulmer, Slough, Bucks.

Talland School of Equitation, Siddington, Cirencester, GL7 6EZ.

Crabbet Park Equitation Limited, Worth, Crawley, Sussex.

Gracious Pond Stables, Chobham, Surrey.

COMPETITIONS

British Show Jumping Association and British Horse Society, National Equestrian Centre, Kenilworth, War., CV8 2LR.

ACKNOWLEDGEMENTS

THE collection of material for this book would not have been possible without the help of a very large number of people. Nearly everybody mentioned in the text gave up their time for discussions and sometimes to train me, but there are some to whom I owe even more—Charles Harris and Lars Sederholm who gave me suggestions before I started; Countess Nadine Redwich, and Edouard Pictet who were particularly helpful in getting interviews and training sessions; Colonel Nyblaeus, Domini Lawrence, Dr. Jean Claude Bouffault, Peter and Krag Andersen who read and improved parts of the text; Jill Miller who deciphered my manuscript to type out the book; and my parents for both their encouragement and criticisms.

INDEX